Walter A. Ratcliffe

Morning Songs in the Night

Poems

Walter A. Ratcliffe

Morning Songs in the Night
Poems

ISBN/EAN: 9783744713986

Printed in Europe, USA, Canada, Australia, Japan

Cover: Foto ©Thomas Meinert / pixelio.de

More available books at **www.hansebooks.com**

MORNING SONGS

IN THE NIGHT

Poems

BY

WALTER A. RATCLIFFE

WITH A PREFACE BY

WILLIAM DOUW LIGHTHALL, M.A., F.R.S.L.
MONTREAL

TORONTO:
WILLIAM BRIGGS
WESLEY BUILDINGS

MONTREAL: C. W. COATES.   HALIFAX: S. F. HUESTIS.

1897

TO THE MEMORY

OF HIS RECENTLY DEPARTED FRIEND

Mrs. R. M. Wilson

OF LISTOWEL, ONT.

WHO FOR MORE THAN THREE YEARS WAS A MOTHER TO THE

AUTHOR, AND UNDER WHOSE ROOF MOST OF

THESE "SONGS" WERE WRITTEN

THIS BOOK IS AFFECTIONATELY AND REVERENTLY

DEDICATED BY

THE AUTHOR.

LISTOWEL, *April, 1897.*

PREFACE.

WITHIN these covers is to be found one of the most notable volumes of verse recently published in Canada, because probably no other deals so intensely yet simply with the everyday problems of the soul and of suffering humanity. The author, Walter A. Ratcliffe, of Listowel, Ontario, has for years been cut off from the ordinary pleasures of life by an unusually heavy affliction—having become almost totally blind and deaf. His only communication with his few friends has been through the ear trumpet and the sympathetic touch and treatment. In the sadness of his life his poetry has been to him a solace and an unburdening, and we catch the heart-throbs in the singing of the caged linnet:

> "If I should die to-night
> No terror would affright;
> No quailing at the billows' ceaseless boom,
> No boding fear of boundless, rayless gloom,
> And chill and damp of night.
> But when the last warm light
> Of life, a burned-out candle's glow,
> Shines o'er the fleeted years, what would it show,
> If I should die to-night?"

Brooding such thoughts, he turns with a bond of deep sympathy to the sufferings of the masses of mankind; sees them bear the fetters of ceaseless toil and reap only a fraction of its fruits, while the wealthy revel in vastly disproportionate luxury; sees, in most countries, their poverty made hopeless by great monopolies of land; and he sings of a coming era when these injustices and monopolies shall disappear, and mankind—and especially the sons and daughters of his country—shall be free:

> "Free from the thraldom of gold,
> Free from the wars of their creeds,
> Free from the terror of want,
> Free with the freedom of Love."

His leanings find a remedy for much in a socialistic order of society—perhaps too much, for how can any legislation from without produce an ideal society without a regeneration from within?

Death and the future life are subjects of intense probing by him; not wild nor fanciful, but the piercings of a thoughtful mind and balanced judgment:

> "Like glow-worms that, in perfume-laden June,
> A moment gleam where vines have hid the moon;
> Or, like the prismic hues on bubbles fair,
> A moment bright,—a touch, a breath, then where?
> Or like the wand'ring stars o'er heaven's face,
> That flit as flits a smile, then melt in space:
> We come and go, we know not whence or why,
> And call it Life, this moment's laugh and sigh.

> "The oriole's trilling in the poplar shade,
> The pearly dew-drop on the thirsting blade,
> Yon fairy form, sun-kist at eve and free,
> A snow-drift sailing in an azure sea,—
> If these be vain, if these be worthless quite,
> Then, only then, meseems thou saidst aright.

> "Far 'neath the restless wave an insect train,
> Unseen, unheard, doth toil, yet not in vain;
> Each walls its little cell, and roofs it o'er,
> Then others come and find foundation sure
> Whereon to build; and thus tier over tier
> Is rear'd as Time doth add year unto year;
> *But who first wrought his labor hath not done*
> *Till that fair reef looks forth upon the sun.*
> *So we, my friend, do build, or great or small,*
> *Till Error dies and Truth is all in all.*"

In style, the quiet force of many of Mr. Ratcliffe's lines, their frequent happiness of phrase or metaphor, as in those just quoted, strike one. Not that they often come very near the word-wealth of the art-poets, the exquisite music of the lyrists, the fastidious culture of the classicists, or the profundity of the metaphysical specialist; but in clear intelligence and plain good taste they take excellent rank, and few current volumes will be found to contain so many poems which leave the reader earnestly thinking. The author has evidently a sure hold on higher comfort, but it ought to be one source of happiness to him that he can so vigorously sing and teach as to be probably fulfilling a more useful place than the average individual of unimpaired faculties, and that this little work will go on singing and teaching long after him. Perhaps he has been sentinelled at one of the outposts of misfortune to show how bravely misfortune can be borne.

W. D. LIGHTHALL.

"*Chateauclair*," *Westmount, Montreal.*

CONTENTS.

	PAGE
Sunset	13
The River	15
Evening and Morning	17
The Coming Kingdom	19
Canada's Autumn	21
Victory	23
Laurier	24
The River's Lesson	25
The Storm is Over	28
The Sower	29
Man Was Not Made to Sigh	31
Angels of Dawn	32
There's a Glimmer	34
How Little We Know	35
Moonlight in Medonte	36
In the Twilight	37
In the Gloaming	38
Waiting	39

CONTENTS.

	PAGE
HERE AND NOW	41
IN MEMORIAM	42
ON THE ST. LAWRENCE	44
JESSIE	46
THE GOLDEN PAVEMENT	47
THE NEW YEAR	48
TO THE MARCH WIND	49
THE POOR MAN'S HERITAGE	51
LOVE	52
TWO HANDS	53
THE DAY IS AT HAND	55
THIS WORLD OWES YOU NOTHING	57
HELL	59
SONS OF CANADA, AWAKE!	61
TO THE KING	63
EVERLASTING LIFE	65
SELFISHNESS	67
FAIR-WEATHER FRIENDS	68
LOOKING BACKWARD	69
THERE'S A BRIGHT DAY COMING	72
LIFE'S STREAM	74
ONLY ONE AT A TIME	76
WHO WOULD NOT DIE?	77
WHAT LIES BEYOND?	78
ONE IN TWO	79
THEY MET AS STRANGERS MEET	80
WHO IS WEAK?	81
THE FORD	83
IF I SHOULD DIE TO-NIGHT	85
WHEN THE REAPER COMES	87
THE SQUIRE AND THE BEES	88
WANTED, A MAN	90

CONTENTS.

	PAGE
ANSWERED PRAYER	92
A SERMON	94
THE LAND MONOPOLIST	96
TRUTH, UPHOLD AND GUIDE ME	97
NOT ALL	98
THOU HAST NOT	99
NIGHT	100
LIFE	101
WHEN I FOLD MY HANDS	102
THE SONG OF THE STORM KING	103
ON LIFE'S OCEAN	105
THE AWAKENING	107
TO CANADA	109
IT MIGHT HAVE BEEN	111
LIFE	113
TO GRANDMA	114
THE FROST	116
NOVEMBER	118
ON THE SHORE I STOOD AT EVEN	120
A CHRISTMAS SONG	122
THOU LORD SEEST ME	123
THE OLD YEAR AND THE NEW	124
LIFE'S BATTLE-FIELD	126
A VISION OF HELL	128
NORMA	131

SUNSET.

The clam'rous, careful day is well-nigh done.
Above the lake's bright brim th' unwearying sun,
As one who would not quit a pathway bright,
Seems loit'ring, loath to leave the earth to-night.
The east hills blush as maids when lovers woo;
A changeful path of rubies, gold and blue,
Lies o'er the calm lake's gently heaving breast,
And slowly melts into the glowing west.
The frog's shrill piping in the brook below,
The homeward cawing of the vagrant crow,
The lane-bar's clatter, and the cow-bell's song,
The soft wind's sigh, the trailing vines among,—
All speak the hour when carking cares should cease;
All speak the night's repose, the calm of peace.

I watch the spectral gloom o'er woodland fall;
I list the whip-poor-will's loud pensive call.
As brooding night stoops low, and yet more low,
My soul is pressed by mingled joy and woe;
For pleasure lightly treads amid the pain,
As gleams the fitful sunshine through the rain.

I see the path of life, its ills recall,
Behold its sun decline, its shadows fall;
I see dark pitfalls gape where men must tread;
I see the stones that weary feet have bled.
All down his path a bandit robber band
Beset way-faring man on every hand,—
Dejection, Disappointment, dark Despair,
Misfortune multiplied, false Friendship fair,
Love unrequited, fond Ambition crushed,
Hope so deferred that e'en her voice is hushed,—
All vex him till he hates his every breath,
And sighs impatient for the hand of Death.

Yet Death is overcome e'en at the grave,
For Life is queen and he her vassal-slave.
The woodland vet'rans totter where he breathes;
But o'er their prostrate forms Life gently wreathes
With each returning spring green garlands fair,
And sows her sweet forget-me-nots with care.

'Gainst mortal foes, sweet Patience, work thy will!
Shine, Star of Hope, across man's pathway still!
For Life and Light his weary soul may crown,
When from the western hills his sun goes down.

THE RIVER.

Far back among the woody hills,
    In some secluded nook
Where springs give birth to limpid rills,
    Was born a tiny brook,
From out whose banks forget-me-nots
    And bright-eyed violets look.

It babbles down the steep incline,
    It murmurs through the dale,
Here checkered by the sun and vine,
    There rippled by the gale;
Anon joined by some other brook
    From out some other vale.

Thus fed by other streams, it grows
    More quiet, still as free
As when a brook the river flows
    Toward the bounding sea,
Resistless in its quiet might,
    Yet not so full of glee.

Here narrowed by approaching shores
   In angry haste it leaps,
There silently it onward pours
   In dark unbroken deeps,
Or loiters by some wid'ning lake
   Where drooping willow weeps.

Just so our life! Its youthful glee
   Grows less as years speed on;
The joyous laugh, from care so free,
   Trust, known to youth alone,
And the pure heart of innocence,
   Are all too quickly gone.

Soon trials of maturer years
   Like narrowing banks are met,
And sapping sorrows, boding fears,
   Life's onward stream to fret.
How oft along its winding course
   We pause in vain regret!

They forward glide, nor either know
   What falls before them be.
No barrier long may hold them back,
   They must, they will be free;
Through sunshine and through cloud they seek
   Their haven in the sea.

EVENING AND MORNING.

The great sun sinks with an angry flush;
   Like billows of smoke the dark clouds toss
And roll and surge till, a dusky pall,
   They droop the roofless dome across.
The stars are hid, and the moon smiles not
   Thro' the veil that is draped from the hemlocks' spires;
The night-winds sleep in the hill-lands' heart;
   Hushed are the strains of their phantom lyres.

Out of the West the Snow-sprite comes;
   Light as the down of the thistle she soars,
Sifting her frozen flowers the while
   O'er wooded upland and treeless moors.
For the knotted arms of the grim old trees
   Fair garlands her magic finger weaves;
Each scar she hides with a wreath more fair
   Than the shimmering folds of their spring-time leaves.

Then, when the night is nearly done,
   And the burdened pines forget to sigh,
And the cedars sleep with arms entwined,
   The hoar-frost stoops from the starry sky:

She breathes on the maple, the beech, the oak,
  And the trailing strands of the shattered vines;
And, gleeful at what the dawn will do,
  She kisses the beards of the sombre pines.

'Tis done, and over the earth's white rim
  Stretch the ruby fingers of smiling Dawn,
Till, a Midas, he touches each blossom and spray,
  By lake and by river, on upland and lawn.
The woods awake with a murmur low;
  Higher the great sun rides and higher,
Till the trees flash back his fervent glow
  From a million points of frozen fire.

THE COMING KINGDOM.

I've sailed the dancing waters,
  I've trod the golden strand,
I've spoke the sons and daughters
  Of that enchanted land;
I've drunken of her fountains,
  The sweetest and the best;
I've rambled o'er her mountains,
  I've revelled in her rest.

Enslaving Superstition
  Her sunny shore hath fled;
Blind bowing to Tradition
  Is dead—forever dead;
Time-honored landmarks hoary,
  With ivy overgrown,
Are buried with their glory
  When truer guides are known.

Within her spacious borders
  No needy man I found,
No aimless idle hoarders,
  No gentle woman bound;

There Truth is more than treasure,
    And Love the scales doth hold;
There Mercy hath no measure,
    And Man is more than Gold.

No war-god ever mutters
    His bloody mandate there;
No battle banner flutters
    Upon her balmy air;
For nation loveth nation
    As man his fellow can,
Her honor and salvation
    The brotherhood of man.

The gray old world rolls onward
    Through all the changing years,
And upward, ever upward,
    Through sacrifice and tears;
What others sowed in sorrow
    We garner while they sleep,
And labor for to-morrow
    That others, too, may reap.

That land is straight before us:
    Oh, hail her, Star of Morn!
Come, join the joyous chorus
    Of sons to Freedom born.
Come, help each burdened nation
    From sorrow find surcease
In world-wide federation,
    An everlasting peace.

CANADA'S AUTUMN.

Autumn, sturdy Autumn,
Prince of all the seasons,
Very soul of gladness,
Thou art ever welcome
For the joy thou bringest.

Summer saw thee coming.
Lovingly she loitered,
Walked with thee till even,
Tho' thy feet we heard not;
Then when sunset arrows
Quivered in the tree-tops,
With a sigh she left us,
Leaving thee her sceptre.

Not till on the morrow
Knew we of thy coming;
Then the lordly maple
Waved aloft thy standard.

Now in thee, O Autumn,
Clad in all thy glory,
Clad in brilliant beauty,
See we Joy unceasing.

Thine's a gleaming glory,
Regal pomp and splendor;
All thy host is knightly;
All the hoary giant
Monarchs of the greenwood,
Marshalled in thy honor,
In their glowing armor,
Flash their gladsome greeting
From each glen and hill-top:

Crimson, gold and purple,
Green and shimmering silver,
All give back the sunshine
Of thy joyous smiling.

And the bow of heaven,
Thousand-tinted rainbow,
Is the arch triumphal
Through which thou art marching.

In the golden sunrise
And the purple even,
Rise from off thy altars
Smoke of burning incense,
Till the earth is shrouded
In a veil of amber.
Strains of dreamy music,
As of some sweet anthem
By thy choir, hidden
In the forest's bosom,
Float adown the valley,
Dying on the hill-tops.

Plenty thou hast brought us;
Joy is with thy bounty;
We would have thee tarry,—
Hasten not to leave us.

VICTORY.

Sing, ye mighty hills, in chorus!
    Sing, ye torrents free and strong!
Gleeful rills, in silv'ry trebles,
    Swell the universal song—
Not of triumph over Party,
    But of triumph over Wrong!

Sing, ye sons of this our country!
    Shout aloud from wave to wave!
Tyranny and foul corruption
    Now are sleeping in their grave.
Canada hath loudly spoken:
    Truth and justice she will have.

Wake to greet the golden dawning
    That shall follow twilight gray;
Rustles now the breeze of morning,—
    Lo! our night has rolled away!
Worthy sons of worthy sires,
    Welcome in the fuller day,

When no mandate of the many
    Shall oppress the feebler few;
When the worthy shall be honored,
    And the weak receive his due,
And the bosom of the nation
    Harbor only what is true.

LAURIER.

Stout heart and free, more glorious in defeat
   Than they who triumph o'er eternal right,
Upon the scroll of Fame, where patriots meet,
   Thy name is writ, a deathless name of light.
   As giant maple on some crested height,
Thou standest proof 'gainst tempest's thund'ring shock,
Firm as the base of Hochelaga's rock,
   Pledge of our glorious country's honest might.
   Fair Canada shall ever more delight
To name thee fairest of her sons true-born,
Her star of Hope, her radiant star of morn,
   Triumphant o'er Corruption's shame and blight.
When thou hast gone thy way beyond our ken,
Thy noblest shrine, the hearts of honest men.

THE RIVER'S LESSON.

I stood on the brink of a river,
Deep-flowing and broad and majestic,
Watching the sun-gilded ripples
And the bubbles that covered its surface.
Borne on the breast of its current
Came leaves of the forest, and branches,
And logs that were sodden and covered
With rot and with moss and with mildew.
Aimlessly downward they drifted,
Here spun like a top in an eddy,
There turned by the tortuous current.
Ofttimes a tree that had fallen
Prone from the bank to the water,
Its skeleton arms far extending,
Caught all the heaviest driftwood.
These as they lay unresisting
Hindered the others from passing;
So were the leaves of the forest,
The logs and the branches and bubbles,
Held by the skeleton fingers
Of a form that for long had been lifeless.

Fretted they not at their bondage,
But listlessly jostled each other,
Till from the hill-lands afar off,
Home of the broad river's fountains,
Thundered a freshet, dark-surging,
That carried them over their keeper,
Or, sweeping the bank in its fury,
Hurried it downward before him.
Then forward, or backward, or sidewise,
All of them drifted together,
Anyway, so without effort
They might their journey accomplish.

Thus did I stand by the river,
Watching the leaves of the forest,
The logs and the branches and bubbles,
Borne by its will unresisted
Down to the slime of the marshes,
Till weary I grew of the sameness.
But as I turned from the river,
The sound of the plash of a paddle
Grew clear and more clear as I listened,
And, rounding a point of the forest,
Far into the water projecting,
Came unattended a Boatman.

Not with the others he drifted,
But bravely he breasted the current.
Bronzed were his arms and his shoulders;
With sweat that was born of his toiling,
Thickly his temples were beaded.
Forward he went with a purpose,
Learning the depth of the river,
Testing the strength of the current,

Marking the rocks as he passed them.
Ever unaided, but hindered
By those who were borne by the current,
Patiently upward he journeyed
In search of the far-away hill-lands,
Home of the broad river-fountains.
And the leaves of the forest, the branches
And logs, in their moss and their mildew,
Laughed at the Boatman who labored
While they were borne carelessly onward.

Go, list to the voice of the River,
As under its shadows it whispers,
And learn ye the lesson it teaches.

THE STORM IS OVER.

Last night the heavens scowled, the moon was hid,
   No beaming star looked forth to light the gloom;
The billows, storm-tossed, broke upon the strand
   With ceaseless boom;
The tempest's icy breath was o'er the lea:
   The driving snow, a million-pointed cloud,
Swept over land and sea;
   The cold wind wildly wailed, and loud;
      But to-day the storm is over.

Last night the knotted arms of vet'ran trees
   Were tossed and torn with many a grinding groan:
Anon a giant fell, they hailed his fall
   With mournful moan.
Loud shrieked the gale among the bearded pines;
   The last leaves from their twisted twigs were torn,
And sere, dishevelled vines;
   But all is bright and fair this morn,
      For to-day the storm is over.

THE SOWER.

A sower went forth to sow,
   For the April sun and rain
Had warmed and softened the earth,
   And made it ready for grain;
So he toiled in patience and hope
   While May was spreading her leaves,
And great was his joy at the reaping-time
   Over his golden sheaves.

Another went forth to sow,
   But he loitered by the way;
He scattered no seed abroad
   Till past was the seeding-day;
But when he went forth to reap
   And bind his grain in sheaves,
He had no joy, for he carried home
   Only a handful of leaves.

Now is the seeding-time,
   This world the open field,
If the sower sow good seed
   'Twill abundant harvest yield.

The sower may labor in want,
   He over each furrow may weep,
He may sleep ere the harvest sun shall rise,
   But another shall surely reap.

Then scatter no seed by the way
   But that which is pure and good,
For know that the harvest to be
   Will be garner'd by reapers for food;
So toil that when others shall eat,
   They may not in bitterness say:
"Our bread is defiled, for with thistles and tares
   He cumbered the earth in his day."

MAN WAS NOT MADE TO SIGH.

MAN was not made to sigh and moan,
   Life's all too short for gloomy sorrow;
Yet oft his song is but a groan,
   If sad to-day, more sad to-morrow.

The rills make music all day long,
   The sun's bright smile each ripple stealing;
The green old woods are full of song,
   Like childhood's mirthful laughter pealing.

'Tis only man who will be sad,
   When earth and sea and sky are smiling;
How oft he deems he sins if glad,
   And duly mourns his soul's defiling.

One winter day is Life to these,
   No Spring can melt the bonds that bound them;
In sight of glowing coals they freeze,
   And chill the hearts of all around them.

Then let us sing tho' tempests howl,
   The sun behind the hills is shining;
We'll laugh when clouds the blackest scowl,
   And rend them for their golden lining.

ANGELS OF DAWN.

BEAUTIFUL Spirits of Light
  Waking the Ruby Dawn,
Radiant offspring of Night,
  Breathing o'er hillside and lawn
    Love never-dying and Peace,
    From ev'ry Sorrow surcease,
    And thraldom of Wrong release,
      Angels of Dawn.

Come ere the glare of day
  Burst on our waking eyes;
Bid ye our thoughts alway
  On pure wings to rise;
    Our wayward lips then close,
    Keep ye the gates of those,
    Lest they should prove our foes,
      Angels of Dawn.

As through the day we move,
  Leave not, but linger nigh;
Show us the hand of Love
  On lake and hill and sky;

So teach us self to shun,
That, ere the light is gone,
Some good by us be done,
　　Angels of Dawn.

And through the darksome night
　Watch till the morrow's morn;
Greet us again with light,
　New love with day be born;
　　So through each changing year
　　Come and be ever near,
　　Be ours to warn and cheer,
　　　Angels of Dawn.

THERE'S A GLIMMER.

There's a glimmer as of dawn
   Trembling in the eastern sky;
See, the night is nearly gone!
   Courage, brothers, day is nigh!
Glorious morn we long have waited,
   Joyous morn of jubilee,—
Brothers, cheer, the day is breaking
   When the people shall be free!

When that day's unclouded sun
   Shines upon the ransomed soil,
Man will cease to plead with man
   For the privilege to toil;
Brothers, cheer, want shall not 'press you,
   Winter shall not make you dread,
You will not then need to labor
   Day and night for daily bread.

Charity shall quench her spark,
   Justice to her throne return,
Room be found for all to work,
   All receive the wage they earn;
Bounty bought with toilers' wages
   In that day shall seem not good,
Brothers, cheer, that day is dawning,
   Legal theft shall be subdued!

HOW LITTLE WE KNOW.

Of the past that is gone, of the present that is,
   Of the tide of this life with its ebb and its flow,
Of the times that shall be when life's journey is done,
   How little we know—oh, how little we know!

Oft a brother goes down in the way he has trod,
   And we bid him arise as we deal him a blow;
We see his defeat, but the foes that he fought
   We never can know—no, we never can know!

Of the heart fiercely torn by relentless Remorse,
   Of the tears all in vain that in secret may flow,
Of the wounds we may make when our brother we spurn,
   We seek not to know—oh, we seek not to know!

Of the hopes that are thwarted, the fears that assail,
   Of the yearnings that cry from the blackness of woe,
Of the struggle unaided, the strife all alone,
   How little we know—yes, or seek we to know!

Yet we judge in our pride, and condemn; for we stand
   Where we think Wisdom's beacon is shedding her glow;
But how soon we may fall, than our brother more low,
   How little we know—oh, how little we know!

MOONLIGHT IN MEDONTE.

When day has fled and the night's long shadows
    Have shrouded the earth in a sombre pall,
Ere the moon comes out above the meadows,
    A sweet, soft silence reigns over all.

The fire-flies flash and then are hidden,—
    Noiseless as sprites on their way they move;
Luminous tapers, unheard, unbidden,
    Sparkle like gems in the dome above.

Then the moon, with her shining sandals soundless,
    Glides like a bride 'cross the threshold of Night,
And with a smile so effulgent and boundless,
    Changes earth's darkness to radiant light.

The South-wind warbles from lutes without number,
    Slumbrous chords vibrate to fingers unseen,
The myriad leaves awake from their slumber
    And whisper their love to the Night's fair Queen.

Beauteous Night! Thou hast nothing to mar thee;
    Love is thy soul and thy song too is Love;
Nothing discordant hath place here to jar thee,
    Peace, dreamy peace, all around and above.

IN THE TWILIGHT.

As I sat in the gath'ring twilight,
    Pensive, and musing alone,
Methought that the Night-wind whispered,
    "All things are going, are gone."

And it seemed that the whisper grew clearer
    Till my heart caught the mournful refrain,
And I felt as the shadows grew deeper,
    Life's battle is surely in vain.

For I know that each light has its shadow,
    That each pleasure is followed by pain,
And the friends of to-day on the morrow
    Are parted to meet not again.

While the hopes that are born in the morning
    Lie low 'neath the dew of the night,
And the hearts that beat warmest and strongest
    Are soonest to plume them for flight.

And the life that we treasure, as misers
    Treasure their silver and gold,
Must wane, just as waneth the twilight,
    For the darkness of Death so cold.

But each night that hath fled had its morning,
    And perchance, when that night has flown,
We shall open our eyes to the dawning
    Of a sun that shall never go down.

IN THE GLOAMING.

BRIGHT is the sunshine, and glad the day's music,
    But the heart, weary, seeks not for rest,
Till the trees on the east hills, crowned with red glory,
    Smile at the shadows fast shrouding the west.

How sweet is the hour as the shadows grow longer
    And the last golden sunbeams die flickering away,
And the sentinel pine-trees their plumes droop in silence,
    While Night drapes the Earth for the death of the day.

And oft a sweet sadness comes over me stealing,
    As I dreamily muse on the things that have been,
And longingly, yearningly dream of what may be,
    In the Future that's hid by a curtain so thin.

But the North-wind sweeps sighing through tall leafless
        poplars,
    And I start at the gloom, for the last light has fled,
And the breeze bears a whisper, "Men read not the Future,
    And no word ever comes to this world from the Dead."

WAITING.

Waiting in Life's rosy morning fair,
  By the garden wall of Time they wait,
Reckless that the weeds are growing there,
  While they listless swing upon the gate;
Reckless that the fairest flowers droop and die,
While they wonder at the blueness of the sky.

Waiting when the sun is overhead,
  Dreaming of a day beyond the blue,
Heedless that the deadly ivy spread,
  Heedless that the thorns and thistles grew,
While the moments of their morning rolled away
Like the dew-drops from the grass in sunny May.

Waiting in the quiet afternoon
  When the sun has nearly crossed the dome;
Smiling at the early rising moon,
  Waiting when the bee is coming home;
They are waiting while the shadows gather deep,
They are waiting till their eyes are closed in sleep.

WAITING.

Waiting, they are waiting all the day,
   So the garden still is overgrown;
For they cut no cumb'ring weed away,
   From its paths they carry not a stone;
Bear they to the fainting flowers no water sweet,
Raise for them no shelter from the noontide heat.

Cease we waiting while the sunlight beams;
   Cease we waiting ere the twilight's gray;
Cease we dreaming empty, idle dreams;
   Let no hand be idle while 'tis day.
In Time's garden none may labor in the night,
For the skilful workman needs must have the light.

HERE AND NOW.

YE who are strong as the pines on the mountains,
    Boast not; ye stand in the shadow of Death.
Night follows Noontide, as Noontide the Dawning;
    Man is as grass, and his life but a breath.

Ye who are weak, murmur not at your weakness;
    Deem not the moment ye live of no worth.
Go to the brook-side and learn of the violets;
    Many rejoiced in the day of their birth.

All are at one, then; the weakest, the strongest,
    All must go down in the way that they tread;
Theirs are the hands that have labored the longest,
    That toiled for the living unheeding the dead.

Who can be just when the Leveller has claimed him?
    Who can repay from the Valley of Gloom?
Who can repent in the Sepulchre's silence?
    Who can take thought to do good in the Tomb?

Would ye be young when to-day is called ancient?
    Would ye be loved in the ages to be?
Gird for the battle, nor rest from the conflict
    Of Here and Now till the nations are free.

IN MEMORIAM.

W. G. HAY, DIED JANUARY 27, 1896.

Out from yon echoless shore,
Out from yon shadowy bourne,
Over the billowy tide
Dark rolling between us and them,
Swift as the wings of the wind,
Silent as night soaring down,
Hastened a shadowy bark.
Sightless the boatman and old,
Pulseless the heart in his breast,
Ice than his fingers less cold,
But he found thee and called thee to rest.
And thou with a smile heardst his call;
Thou, gentle father revered,
Husband and brother and friend,
Pillowed thy head on his breast,
And he wafted thee over the tide
Into the gloom of the night.
Back through the mist of our tears,
Over thy pathway of life

Looking, thy footprints we see
Ever where duty has led.
There fadeless blossoms of Love
Spring, smiling, to tell of the hand
That succored the needy and lone.
If thou didst err by the way,
Thy zeal for the truth was at fault,
And love hath the error redeemed.
Then rest, weary brother, in peace,
While we tarry in patience and hope
For the boatman to pilot us hence.

ON THE ST. LAWRENCE.

PLACIDLY mighty St. Lawrence
Glides from the portal of even,
Forth to the rolling Atlantic,
   Forth to the heart of the sea;
Like to a soul never selfish,
Buoyant and gentle, yet noble,
Bearing the burdens of others,
   Strong in the strength of the free.

Tarries the sun for a moment,
'Neath curtains of purple and crimson,
Just on the threshold of amber
   And gold of the Gates of the West,
Smiling a smile of approval:
Then drops from his warm, shining fingers
Showers of rarest of rubies,
   Gems for that tide's rippled breast.

Fair, in the flush of that glory,
Kissed by the lips of the river,
Fann'd by the breath of the East-wind,
   Revels the emerald island.
Forth from the stately Cathedral,
Beautiful poem in marble,

Gently the Hymn of the Even
   Floats over valley and highland.

Softly the voice of the Sister,
The laughter and glee of the children,
Like prattle of streamlets in Spring-time
   Come to us sweet as we pass—
Sweet as the call of the robin,
Sweet as the song of the South-wind,
Sweet as the Hymn of the Harpers
   Over the billows of glass.

Forward we float with the river,
Out of the vanishing glory,
Into the shadows that gather,
   Till the sweet voice of the Sister,
The laughter and glee of the children,
   Seem but a wail and a moan,
And the beautiful temple of marble
   Only a dungeon of stone,
Reared on the backs of the toilers,
Crushing the hearts of the builders,
   Till Hope from her temple had flown
For up in the heart of the city
They languish in numberless hovels,
   Where sunshine and joy are unknown.

Perishless Love, never changing,
Come to the heart of our Country,
Breathe o'er each prairie and mountain,
   And banish the gloom of our Night;
Sweep by thy might from our cities
Tenements shadowed by temples,
Be thou for Hearth and for Altar,
   And for the Nation the Light.

"JESSIE."

[Written on the occasion of the unveiling of the monument erected to the memory of Jessie Keith.]

As tender flower, that from each wind unkind
   We shield with watchful care,
In home's sweet garland love so gently twined,
   She daily grew more fair.

But as untimely frosts in balmy spring
   Upon the flowers come,
Chill Death by Jessie stayed his soundless wing
   And bore her from that home.

She prized—oh, joy 'mid grief's tempestuous gloom—
   Her honor more than life,
Viewed undismayed her all too early tomb,
   And fell in that red strife.

This pulseless stone, the passing stranger's tear,
   October's sighing breath,
Henceforth shall teach our hearts to daily fear
   Dishonor more than death.

THE GOLDEN PAVEMENT.

OLD Father Time speeds onward,
   As noiseless as the spheres,
Each pathway swiftly paving
   With precious golden years.

To some he gives full many,
   To others but a few;
To each way-farer trusting
   To keep their setting true.

Time surely lays the pavement,
   But he who treads it needs
Must burnish it, or tarnish,
   With good or evil deeds.

Thy pathway may be hidden
   In shadows as of night;
But know that gems most precious
   Are farthest from the light;

And know yon stately river
   Is fed by tiny rills,
That, long unheard, unnoticed,
   Creep gurgling from the hills.

Then deem upon thy pavement
   No task too mean or light,
That those who follow find it
   A pathway up to Right.

THE NEW YEAR.

At thy feet hoary Time lays the year,
A book bound in sunshine of promise;
Each leaf is of silver refined,
Ruled, margin'd and ready for writing.
In the night as thou sleepest he turneth
Backward the page that is written,
And seals it in silence forever;
So thou canst in nowise re-turn it,
If thou hast left aught unrecorded,
Or a blot thou wouldst cleanse from its surface.
One page at a time is thy portion;
So be not impatient, but careful
To fill it from margin to margin,
Each letter with love to illumine.
Ay, cover with truth and with kindness
Each page of the book that thou writest,
That all who shall read o'er thy shoulder
May treasure thy words with rejoicing.

TO THE MARCH WIND.

WILD Breath of March, fierce Breath of March,
    The ever free, the ever strong,
While minstrels sing of softer airs,
    Thou too art worthy of a song.
I leave their lays to gentler bards;
    Thou herald of returning Spring,
Thou last of Winter's giant host,
    Free Breath of March, 'tis thee I sing!

Like love-lorn maids the zephyrs sigh,
    By shadow'd lake in sylvan glen,
Or murmur low Earth's even-song;
    Thou searchest out the haunts of men:
Thro' crowded city thoroughfare,
    Broad avenue, dim alley gray,
Out o'er the swollen surging sea,
    Thou speedest on thy cleansing way.

Free Breath of March, strong Breath of March
    Blow through the nation's sounding halls,
Blow out the scheming, seeming cant,
    Blow out the politicians' brawls.

Blow out the strife of rival creeds;
    Blow out the thought of carnage red,
The ever-present fear of Want,
    The plaintive wail for daily bread.

Speed round our globe, free Breath of March,
    From pole to pole, from sea to sea:
From cliff to crag, in thunder tones,
    Go, bid the nations to be free;
Go, quench the wasting fire of hate
    Beneath thy swiftly-driving snow;
Blow into flame Love's embers bright,
    Till all the Earth shall feel her glow.

THE POOR MAN'S HERITAGE.

Toil, when a tender child;
  Toil, when his arm is strong;
Toil, to the bound of life,
  Be that life short or long;
Want, though his strength be great;
  Want, though his sweat flow free:
These are his right by law,
  These he may hold in fee.

Shame,—if 'tis shame to toil,—
  Ignorance, squalor, grime,
Home that was ne'er a home,
  Babes that are heirs to crime.
His is the right to cringe,
  Sue for a scanty crust,
Right to be glad he may breathe,—
  These he may hold in trust.

E'en when he lays him down
  To sleep his last sleep cold,
He may not rest in peace,
  He still is slave to gold;
His fate the surgeon's board—
  What right have such to graves?
No poor man might be born
  Did rich men not need slaves.

LOVE.

'Tis false that she is dead! She lives, I trow:
   I see her hand upon yon sunset sky;
I feel her breath upon my fevered brow;
   'Tis her sweet voice that whispers softly nigh.
Her name is written in the daisy's eye;
   O'er heaven's dome in diamond points of light;
'Tis sung by joyous brooks that gambol by;
   'Tis blazoned on the dark'ning brow of night.
   Tho' erring man hath done her throne despite,
And oft is captive led by Hate's design,
Love still is queen,—she reigns by right divine,
   And lives his rugged path to warm and light.
The moon shall wane, the sun grow dim and cold,
But Love is Love, till Time's long tale is told.

TWO HANDS.

One hand that I saw was large and brown,
    Mis-shapen, and rough, and marr'd ;
'Twas stain'd with the toil of weary years,
    By many a seam 'twas scarr'd ; .
'Twas a strong right hand that had helped to fill .
    The coffers of more than one,
But 'twas crippled by want thro' a dreary life,
    And was empty when life was done.

The *other* I saw was a blue-vein'd hand
    So soft and white and warm,
Bedeck'd by many a shining gem,
    And perfect in beauty and form.
It never knew want, tho' it never had toiled ;
    No scar or seam it bore ;
But it held the keys to the treasures of Earth
    That were won by the toiling poor.

So one man hath millions and one hath a mite,
    One soars while another's downtrod ;
One's life is all sunshine, the other's all night,
    Tho' sons of the same kind God ;

One revels in wealth that he has not earned,
  Claims title as lord of the soil:
That one may be great in the People's land,
  The ninety and nine must toil.

But the ninety and nine shall yet be free,
  For Justice shall plead their cause,
And Greed and Oppression be crushed to Earth
  By nobler and purer laws;
Then Merit shall rule where birth was wont,
  Then Toil of disgrace shall be shorn,
The hands that labor shall then be full
  And the hearts be glad that mourn.

THE DAY IS AT HAND.

It is coming, surely coming!
   Even now I feel the breath
Of the breeze of early morning,
   And I know the Night of Death
That has brooded o'er the nations
   With its bondage and its blight,
As a blotted scroll, is rolling
   Back before the day of Right.

Yes, the day is swiftly coming
   When the slaves shall know their might:
Oh, restore their birthright, brothers,
   Lest their arms be raised to smite;
Lest like some strong mountain torrent,
   Held by bars of straw and sand,
They shall rise and sweep the forgers
   Of their chains from off the land.

Come and see the crust ye fed them
   While they made for you the day;
See their bed, a cheerless bivouac
   By a cold unsheltered way.

But their night is not eternal;
   Sin, and shame, and death, and tears,
Shall not be the toiler's portion
   All the cycles of the years.

They have sown and they shall garner;
   They have wept, but they shall laugh;
In the day adawning, brothers,
   Theirs the wheat and not the chaff.
Shout the glad unselfish gospel
   O'er the land from sea to sea,
That the day is even dawning
   When the bond-slaves shall be free;—

Free to labor, free from hunger,
   Free from pestilence and crime,
Free to soar from mental dungeons
   Thro' the realms of Thought sublime;
Free to hear their gracious Father
   Speak from forest, tide and glen;
Free to tread where Love would lead them;
   Free to live the lives of men.

None can stay the cleansing torrent
   That shall sweep from Earth its Hell;
None can quench the golden Sunlight
   That shall soon the clouds dispel;
For 'tis coming, surely coming,
   Swiftly coming, all to bless;
O'er the earth shall reign triumphant
   Love, and Truth, and Righteousness.

THIS WORLD OWES YOU NOTHING.

This world owes you naught but a corner to toil—
   That it owes you a living's a lie;
But your right is as good to the bountiful soil
   As it is to the sunshine and sky.
Your hands may be bound by monopolists' chains,
   But they're flimsy as vapor and light;
You may shatter them all if you use your own brains,
   And the ballot—your sceptre of might.

In Life's rosy morning be wedded to Truth,
   And keep her your spouse till you die;
Oh! learn it, my boy, in the days of your youth
   That nothing e'er needed a lie.
It may not be easy truth always to tell,
   But once told and the battle is won;
If you lie you are filling a bottomless well,
   And with lying you never are done.

My boy, if you're honest shrink not to be poor,
   You still are a man among men;
Fawn not on the rich if they come to your door,
   They will only despise you again.

A dollar well earned is worth ten as a gift,
    So wait not for any man's shoes;
Toil steadily onward, look not for a lift,
    You may rise by your might if you choose.

Be sure you are right, for with Right as your guide
    You may stand in the face of the world—
You have nothing to fear, you have nothing to hide,
    Tho' jeers from the foolish be hurled.
Your friends may be few, but their love will be strong,
    For they'll honor the man who is true;
The scoffers will read you, and learn before long
    To give honest Merit his due.

Be true to your country, your neighbor, yourself,
    To the death for the Right be brave;
Be nobody's minion—oh! be not a clod
    To be kicked to a dastard's grave.
Let your hands and your heart be the servants of Love,
    So when from yon valley of gloom
Shall beckon the hand that shall lead you to rest,
    Your name shall not sink to the tomb.

HELL.

I DREAMED that I swiftly did journey
    Far over the bright smiling sea,
In search of a country Elysian
    Where man from himself might be free.
Methought that the winds warred together,
    That the white waves in anger did swell,
Till the bark that had borne me was stranded
    On the shore of the Kingdom of Hell.

Fair peach groves and rich purpling vineyards,
    Broad acres of whitening grain,
Spoke a country where no man might hunger,
    Where no man might labor in vain;
Where the rills and the birds and the flowers
    Made joyous each mountain and dell,
And I knew not the word of the stranger
    Who said 'twas the Kingdom of Hell.

But I saw that the ripening harvest
    Was the tyrant lordling's spoil,
That he reaped in his pride the broad acres
    That were sown by the children of toil;

That the poor were the bond-slaves who garnered
  The fruit as it ripening fell ;
That Famine and Plenty were Devils
  That ruled in the Kingdom of Hell.

There woman was woman no longer,
  But only a serf by the way,
Fettered, despised, and dishonored,
  That men might grow rich in a day ;
And I saw while the lambs gaily gamboled
  'Mong daisies that sprinkled the dell,
Or basked in a heaven of sunshine,
  The babes of the poor were in hell.

Hatred was Monarch Almighty,
  Force was chief of his might,
Greed was the queen of his virtues,
  And right could no longer be Right.
There Hunger and Strife were his minions,
  There Reason and Peace might not dwell,
There Hope was forever a stranger,
  For Love has no portion in Hell.

This land is the land that we cherish ;
  Oh ! why is it red with the strife ?
Come ye, her children, who love her,
  And crown her with newness of life !
Come ye, who hate not your brother,
  And list while I name you a spell :
Cease clutching at brands that are burning,
  And quench ye the fires of this Hell.

SONS OF CANADA, AWAKE!

Hark! a call comes through the trees,
Borne upon the autumn breeze,
Answ'ring ev'ry laughing lake,—
Sons of Canada, awake!

Forest gloom and foaming tide,
Placid stream and prairie wide,
Mount and plain from sea to sea,
Sing the anthem of the free!

Lo, our field-encircled shores,
Teeming mines of shining ores,
Cities crowning many a hill,—
Say, oh, say, what lack we still?

Brotherhood! We need it most;
Brotherhood we dare not boast,
While a senseless racial strife
Saps our country's soul of life.

While the bigot's blinding ban
Makes man hate his fellowman,
Vain the hope of those who wait,—
Canada can ne'er be great.

Canada your fathers fed,
'Twas for her your fathers bled;
Creed- nor race-strifes mar your sky,
Why your common land, oh, why?

Perish Briton, perish Gaul!
Sons of Canada, be all!
From your limbs your fetters shake;
Sons of Canada, awake!

TO THE KING.

Oh, come from thy throne in the North-land,
    Marred not by mortal's device;
Come on the wings of the North-wind,
    Armed with thy arrows of ice.
Monarch of Kings, but no terror;
    Tender thy touch—not a sting;
Come thou, the strong to deliver,
    I will be ready, O King!

Come, for my eyes are aweary,
    Heavy and ready to weep;
Dark are the vapors that dim them,
    Come thou and close them in sleep.
Free thou my heart of its aching,
    Longing and yearning in vain;
Come, and in tenderness bear me
    Back to my mother again.

Why shouldst thou tarry till winter?
    Come in the glow of the spring;
Come when the tender buds open,
    Come when the nesting birds sing.

All are as silent as midnight,
    Autumn and summer and spring;
Strong are the bars of my dungeon,
    Come and release me, O King!

Here we but drift in the shadow
    Of mists overhanging the tide;
Here we but longingly linger
    Close to the narrow Divide.
Is there a realm in the distance,
    Of treasures of knowledge untold?
Thou hast the keys of its future,
    Come, and its secrets unfold.

Oh, come from thy throne in the North-land!
    Come from thy temple of snow,
Reared where eternal Aurora
    Burns till the ice-mountains glow;
Tarry not long in thy coming,
    Pause not to temper thy breath;
Cast not thy shadow before thee,
    I will be ready, O Death!

EVERLASTING LIFE.

Like glow-worms that, in perfume-laden June,
A moment gleam where vines have hid the moon;
Or, like the prismic hues on bubbles fair,
A moment bright,—a touch, a breath, then where?
Or like the wand'ring stars, o'er heaven's face,
That flit as flits a smile, then melt in space:
We come and go, we know not whence or why,
And call it Life, this moment's laugh and sigh.

The oriole's trilling in the poplar shade,
The pearly dew-drop on the thirsting blade,
Yon fairy form, sun-kist at eve and free,
A snow-drift sailing in an azure sea,—
If these be vain, if these be worthless quite,
Then, only then, meseems thou saidst aright.

Far 'neath the restless wave an insect train,
Unseen, unheard, doth toil, yet not in vain:
Each walls its little cell, and roofs it o'er,
Then others come and find foundation sure

Whereon to build; and thus tier over tier
Is rear'd as Time doth add year unto year;
But who first wrought his labor hath not done
Till that fair reef looks forth upon the sun.
So we, my friend, do build, or great or small,
Till Error dies and Truth is all in all.

Dost think yon great eternal orb of fire
Wheels o'er his golden way for daily hire?
Dost think the far-off radiant, cluster'd spheres
For wages ring the changes of the years?
Dost think fair Summer's flowers, her feast of song,
Would cease to be, or deem they suffered wrong,
Not having place beyond November's breath,
Not knowing what, if aught, doth follow death?

Of all that be, of all that love the light,
Man must be recompensed to do the right!
So with the golden thread of fond desire,
And that of hope, refined in Sorrow's fire,
He weaves a curtain for the Gate of Gloom,
And names it Life of Rest beyond the tomb.

We know not what shall be, but this is fair,
If we shall live, then we have lived—but where?
Why ask? The weak, the strong, the bond, the free,
Who breathe to-day, are in eternity.
The hoarded strength of ages passed away
Was in the day that died to bear to-day.
Then learn and know, this fleeting day and we
Are each a part of all that is to be.

SELFISHNESS.

When man of old looked forth upon the sky
    He saw, or tho't he saw, the azure dome
With Sun and Moon and Stars go whirling by,
    Each circling round his central earthly home :
All wand'ring lights save Earth,—she might not roam
    To follow them upon their wayward race ;
She held them or forbade them nearer come.
    He saw her fixed, the pivot of all space.
So oft, methinks, we from our narrow place
    See change in all things save ourselves alone ;
See friends grow cold, lament their wayward pace,
    Tho' they were true and we aside had gone.
What mists would melt, what fell illusions flee,
If from enslaving self man might be free.

FAIR-WEATHER FRIENDS.

When no cloud hides thy sun and no rocks frown ahead,
    When no treacherous shallows betide,
When no buffeting gale makes a toy of thy bark,
    And a friend is each current and tide;
When Prosperity stands with thy helm in her hands,
    And thy Haven of Hope full in view;
When thy sails are all set to a breeze that is fair,
    Then thy friends will be many and true.

But when tempests descend and the white billows roll,
    When thy rudder is shattered and lost;
When thy sails are all rent, ev'ry mast by the board,
    And a wreck on Life's ocean thou'rt tost;
When Adversity looms from his wreck's dreary tombs,
    When thy Compass no longer seems true,
On thine own arm depend, for each fair-weather friend
    As a vapor will vanish from view.

LOOKING BACKWARD.

Out of the town to the Poorhouse
The directors did hasten one day
To a very important meeting,
So does the Chronicle say;
For the last old inmate expired
Only the ev'ning before,
And the Poorhouse, as poorhouse, was useless,—
Useless for evermore.
Nowhere in all the wide county,
Or its villages scattered around,
Or the county town, or the other towns,
One needing its shelter was found.
And these men had loved the pauper,
And the half-paid, and oppressed,
And had banded to build him a shelter
Where his weary bones might rest;
So they met in the matron's parlor
On that sad eventful day,
To discuss the case, find a use for the place,
So does the Chronicle say.

In the chair sat His Honor, Donation,
As troubled as were the rest ;
Pale was his cheek when he rose to speak,
And a great sigh heaved his breast.
" My friends " (and he spoke right heavily),
" Long, long have I feared this hour ;
Long have I watched the progress
That the poor have made in power.
They carried through Prohibition,
Without voting upon it twice,
And set good Malthus ahunting
For his Pestilence and Lice.
Now the halls of our Home are silent,
For the waifs are the wards of the State,
And no longer they seek protection
From the rich man and the great ;
And the Gaol on the hill is empty ;
But why should I weary you ?
We have franchised men and women,
To leave us no good to do.
This house is the fruit of our bounty,
But now we may bar its door,
For nowhere in all the county
A pauper is found so poor
As to crave the kindly shelter
Of this once much-sought abode,
Where so many worn-out toilers
Have laid aside their load.
My weary heart 'twould gladden
To see one vagrant's face,—
I would that we lived in China,
Where the poor man knows his place ;
Where waifs and worn-out toilers
Still crawl upon the earth,

And the rich man still is honored
And respected for his birth;
Where the poor man often hungers
In his hovel bare and rude,
And the rich man to him seemeth
As an angel doing good.
Here we're robbed of all our virtues,
And this burden upon our backs
Is placed by that curse of the bountiful rich,—
I refer to the Single Tax."

Then he sank to his seat exhausted,
'Mid tears, and sighs, and groans,
For they saw of their Christian virtues
Only the whitened bones;
But they found no use for the poorhouse,
With all of their talk that day,
So it stood through many a winter blast,
Then crumbled and fell to the earth at last—
So does the Chronicle say.

THERE'S A BRIGHT DAY COMING.

THERE'S a bright day coming, Tom ;
'Twill not delay its coming, Tom ;
  E'en now the clouds are breaking,
    And soon the sun's bright beams,
Now shining on the mountains, Tom—
Just peering o'er the mountains, Tom—
  Will flood our shadowed valley
    With their joyous golden streams.

We've plodded on together, Tom,
Thro' ev'ry sort of weather, Tom ;
  Oft the up-hill path was dreary,
    And the load was heavy too;
But thy voice was always cheery, Tom,
And tho' sometimes worn and weary, Tom,
  My heart was always gladdened
    By thy loyal love and true.

Thy curly locks so brown, Tom,
Have changed for white their brown, Tom,
  For the snows of many winters
    Have whitened o'er thy head ;

But thou'rt just as young to me, Tom,
And just as fair to see, Tom,
   And I love thee just as fondly
    As the gladsome day we wed.

We've had many a happy day, Tom,
And down all our winding way, Tom,
   Love has lightened ev'ry burden
    And made our pathway plain.
Now our days of toil are o'er, Tom,
So we'll rest and toil no more, Tom,
   But thro' all our sunny even
    Dream our youthful dreams again.

LIFE'S STREAM.

The stream is deep and strong and wide,
   No man its surging depths may sound;
No bridge may ever span its tide,
   No ford along its course is found;
No ship its restless waves may plow,
   A thousand whirlpools threaten loss;
A thousand frowning rocks, I trow,
   Will front the boy who dares to cross.

The stream is deep and strong at best,
   But over nigh the farther strand
There lies an island home of rest,
   Where some may even hope to land.
Dread not the threatening rocks that frown,
   Nor whit'ning waves that wildly toss,
On yonder island lies the crown;
   Be brave, my boy, and strive to cross.

'Twere profit small to idly stand
   And count the ripples as they roll,
To weigh the river's worthless sand
   Or seek some undiscovered shoal;

Thou soon or late must test the tide;
   To loiter is to suffer loss;
With willing arm, whate'er betide,
   Strike boldly forth and strive to cross.

Await no mate to lend a hand,
   Each hath as much as he can bear;
'Twere better far to sink or strand
   Than naught to do, than naught to dare.
Thou mayest reach yon isle of rest
   And live thine even on its shore,
Thence hail, upon the billow's crest,
   The Boatman come to waft thee o'er.

ONLY ONE AT A TIME.

Thy task may be heavy and feeble thy hand,
  Do only one thing at a time;
The hardest of rocks may be beaten to sand
  By striking one blow at a time;
Thy efforts, if honest, must surely avail;
Move surely, if slowly, but never say "Fail;"
Waste not precious moments in foolish regret;
Be cheerful and patient and never forget
  'Tis only one thing at a time.

Though thy pathway be thorny and rugged and high,
  Take only one step at a time;
'Twere folly twice foolish to leap it to try;
  Take only one step at a time.
The goal will be gained if thou amble along
And beat every barrier down with a song;
'Twill lengthen thy journey to worry and fret;
Be cheerful and patient and never forget
  'Tis only one step at a time.

Has thy heart grown aweary with toiling and tears?
  'Tis only one day at a time;
Has thy hope been deferred through the long, lonely
   years?
  Live only one day at a time;
The years tho' they linger are still marching on;
The darkest of nights must be followed by dawn;
Rejoicing shall follow thy sorrowing yet;
Be cheerful and patient and never forget
  'Tis only one day at a time.

WHO WOULD NOT DIE?

Who would not die when death means rest
From every pang that rends the breast,—
A rest from sorrow, rest from spite,
A rest of one eternal night?
Life's joys grow dim, then 'scape our view;
They vanish as the glist'ring dew
When morning's sun rides fierce and high:
If such be Life who would not die?

How full is life of toil and pain;
Toil unrewarded, tears in vain,
Hopes born to perish at their birth,
Fears that might crush a god to earth;
Oft darkness hides the noonday sun
Ere half our earthly course is run;
In silent loneliness we sigh;
When Hope has failed who would not die?

Full oft a friend proves but a reed
That breaks when greatest is our need;
Oft Truth appears in Error's guise,
And he as Truth to mortals' eyes;
What rayless clouds are round us rolled
When love's eye dims, love's heart grows cold?
Fond hearts oft bleed when none are nigh;
If love hath fled who would not die?

WHAT LIES BEYOND?

O FIERCE North-wind, whose icy breath
Has mantled all the hills in white,
And lowly laid the flowers in death,
I'd speak awhile with thee to-night.
What lies beyond this troubled Life?
What lies beyond the bound of Time?
Do weary mortals cease from strife,
And rest in some more peaceful clime?

O fierce North-wind, my restless soul
Longs to be free to soar at will!
While endless ages onward roll,
Say, must she wear her fetters still?
When Death shall come with icy hands,
And snap in twain her prison bars,
Say, must she count Time's ceaseless sands
In weal or woe beyond the stars?

O fierce North-wind, that roarest by,
Does Love reach out beyond the Grave?
Will e'er the fount of tears be dry?
Must hate still follow wave on wave?
We know not whence our spirits came,
Why oft a prey to dark Despond;
When Death hath quenched Life's feeble flame,
O fierce North-wind, what lies beyond?

ONE IN TWO.

Just as two mountain torrents,
  Mad rushing down to the sea,
Leaping from crag to canyon
  In anger or in glee;
Perchance at the foot of a cascade
  Swirling within the breast
Of a rockbound pool unfriendly,
  But never, never at rest.

None of the music and laughter
  Of the limpid loit'ring rills;
None of the dreams that they dream
  As they creep 'mong the basking hills:
The two think not of resting;
  The two may not be free
Till from the walls of their last wild gorge
  They leap to the laughing Sea.

So are our spirits, Viola;
  Not as our fellows are we:
Children of fancy they deem us
  For we see not as other men see.
One throbbing soul in two bodies
  On rushing down to the sea,
Trammeled and chafed like the torrents,
  Striving but never free.

THEY MET AS STRANGERS MEET.

They met as strangers meet;
   Each found the counterpart
Of a longing, yearning soul,
   Heart answering to heart.
Both spake a sad farewell;
   Both knew they passed that way
To drift apart like clouds
   Upon a summer day.

In that brief space they loved
   As ne'er they might again;
Both dreamed the same fond dreams,
   Both knew that Hope was vain:
For 'twixt them stretched a gulf,
   Dark rolling, deep and wide;
They might not launch thereon,
   They might not cross its tide.

Oh, tell me, Zephyrs soft,
   When Death has laid them low,
In realms beyond the tomb
   Shall each the other know?
I list, and through the trees
   The South winds softly sigh,
"Love made them ever one,
   And Love may never die."

WHO IS WEAK?

He was strong, as all men are;
All things he could do and dare;
But one day Temptation came,
Kindling Passion's fervent flame:
As the wax before the heat
So he melted at her feet.
By her might she leads him still,
Unresisting, at her will.
For his strength in vain we seek;
Low he fell, for he was weak.

She was weak, the sages said,
Fickle, coy, and eas'ly led;
She to ill should one day come,
She should shame her birth and home.
She Temptation met one day,
All her shield one answer, "Nay!"
Fawning, Falsehood, foul Deceit,
Laid she bleeding at her feet.
Sorely tried was she, and long,
But she stood, for she was strong.

So it was and is to-day,
Though the sages love to say,
"She the weaker vessel is;
Man is strong, the will is his."
Woman stands where man will fall;
He will answer if she call;
If she lead he follows still,
Be the pathway good or ill.
When temptations thickly throng
Man is weak and woman strong.

THE FORD.

It chanced in yonder shady vale,
   One smiling summer day,
While loit'ring by a bubbling brook
   That gamboled on its way,
I spied a joyous, gleeful troop
   Of barefoot boys at play.

From stepping-stone to stepping-stone,
   With many an agile leap
They sprang, or waded through the flood,
   Where it was not too deep:
In crossing to the farther shore
   Each strove his foot to keep.

So, thought I, is the life of man
   With all its griefs and joys;
Ambitions, titles, power and fame
   Are only larger toys;
Time but a broader channel is,
   Men are but older boys.

We may not leap the troubled tide
   Or scan the distant shore;
We may not ford the stream but once,
   But find a footing sure
On stepping-stones of noble lives
   Of those who crossed before.

To gently lead from stage to stage
   A brother weak or lame,
To light the passage of the stream
   With Love's unflickering flame,
To rear at least one stepping-stone,
   Is Life's one end and aim.

IF I SHOULD DIE TO-NIGHT.

If, ere the morrow bright,
The Boatman from yon distant Shore of Shade
Should come and say, "Long time thou here hast stayed,
    Away with me to-night!"
    And far beyond the sight
Of men should waft me out upon the sea,—
Oh! say, what would the written record be,
    If I should die to-night?

    No terror would affright,
No quailing at the billows' ceaseless boom;
No boding fear of boundless, rayless gloom,
    And chill and damp of night.
    But when the last warm light
Of life, a burned-out candle's glow,
Shines o'er the fleeted years, what would it show,
    If I should die to-night?

    Pale, tearful Sorrow's blight,
As frost in June upon the tender flowers,
Full oft descends to pierce these hearts of ours
    And turn our day to night;

Then when all's still and white,
From out his humble place will one draw near,
And say I kissed away one bitter tear,
    If I should die to-night?

    The wide world seeketh light.
The base, the false, the many long have curst
And wanton hid, tho' faint their souls athirst,
    The well-springs from their sight;
    But would one pause to write
That ever I hoar Age or ruddy Youth
Did point to fountains of Eternal Truth,
    If I should die to-night?

    Now reigns the tyrant Might
And crushes low the weak, for he is strong;
With each succeeding sun red-handed Wrong
    Doth triumph over Right.
    But from the hate and spite,
Would one faint voice in falt'ring accents speak,
And say I once was strength unto the weak,
    If I should die to-night?

    Time doth each deed requite,
For Sorrow's crown of thorns is vain regret;
This we may wear, each thorn with tear-drops wet,
    As day gives place to night.
    I would that naught but light
Of Love, of Truth, of Good may round me shine,
No wasted hour reproach this heart of mine,
    If I should die to-night.

WHEN THE REAPER COMES.

WHEN the Reaper comes to reap
Weary souls that sigh and weep,
And far from this dungeon keep
   To another world we've flown,
Will a brighter sun arise?
Will the mists clear from our eyes?
In a light that never dies
   Shall we know as we are known?

Will misunderstanding cease?
Will the captive find release?
For an everlasting peace
   Will he lay his fetters by?
Will the love that here is vain
Burn to waver not again?
And the tears that fall as rain,
   Will they evermore be dry?

Shall we rest for evermore
On some ever-vernal shore,
Where no billows ever roar
   And the tempests all are still?
Or shall we soon return
To another earthen urn,
With a brighter fervor burn,
   And a nobler being thrill?

THE SQUIRE AND THE BEES.

HALF up a hill with stalwart maples crowned,
And at whose foot a silver streamlet wound,
Nigh hid within the shade of lilac trees,
Nestled the cosy home of Squire Rees,
Who thought on naught save honey and his bees.
  The winter long had been, the cold severe
Had filled his heart with many a boding fear;
But April came and wept and went her way,
Leaving her wand to sunny, smiling May,
Who, by her balmy breath and magic powers,
Called forth to life the early buds and flowers.
So back and forth, from hive to blossom bright,
His toiling bees sped on from morn till night.
  It chanced one day the Squire weary grew,
So 'neath a beech tree's shade himself he threw
Upon a mossy mound hard by the stream,
And fell asleep and dreamed a wondrous dream.
He saw his home, his hives, the field, the trees,—
Naught strange in that had he not missed his bees.
With eye and ear he searched for sight or sound,
But of those miscreant bees no trace he found.

THE SQUIRE AND THE BEES.

At last upon a sturdy thistle's crest
He spied a monstrous bee just 'light to rest,
Who thus, without ado, the Squire addressed :
   "Thy bees are gone—to tell thee that no need ;
For which mishap thou needs must thank thy greed,
For thro' the summer hours that backward flew
No idle breath those faithful toilers drew ;
Much honey stored they ere October's breath
Fell on the flowers and laid them low in death.
Yet, all the while, thy hand was 'gainst them turned
To rob them of the food so fairly earned ;
And, so it was, long ere the snow had fled,
The bees were dying for the want of bread."

   "Thro' all those dreary days my bees I fed."

   "Small credit that! 'Twas unfit food for bees,
Which, while they ate, bred in them foul disease.
They had not need of charity, O Squire,
Hadst thou not robbed them of their lawful hire ;
One single hive thou hadst not had to feed
Had not fair Justice been o'ercome by Greed."
This said, he rose and wheeled his droning flight
Across the fields till passed from farthest sight.
   The Squire awoke well pleased to find, I ween,
'Twas but a dream, this he had heard and seen.
By hill, and tree, and stream, he loudly swore
He of their right his bees would rob no more.

WANTED, A MAN.

  Wanted, a stalwart man!
The man, who, when he knows the Right,
The same pursues against all Might;
The man who dares to stand alone
For Conscience' sake when Hope is gone;
Who dares to leave a beaten path,
And live within the light he hath,
Nor shrinks to strike a deadly blow
At Error found in friend or foe:
  This is the stalwart man.

  Wanted, an honest man!
A man may live within the laws,
Or 'scape their grasp through flimsy flaws,
But he who scorns an action mean,
Is honest where he is not seen,
Nor dares advance at others' cost,
Counts all ill-gotten wealth as lost,
Ne'er grudges each his fullest due,
Whose word as is his oath is true:
  This is the honest man.

Wanted, a noble man!
Not one who from a favored place
Claims kindred with a worn-out race;
Whose empty titles, ancient name,
Are all his wealth, are all his fame;
But one whose usefulness men see,
Though humble may his station be;
For such will bless on every hand
His friend, his home, his native land:
    This is the noble man.

Wanted, the broader man!
Untrammeled by a narrow creed
That loves to make its doubters bleed;
The man who learns from Nature's plan
That man should love his fellowman;
The man whose soul, so deep and true,
Embraces all as brothers too;
The man whom none may buy with pelf,
The man delivered from himself;
    Such is the needed man.

ANSWERED PRAYER.

The lake's long billows broke upon their shingle
Hard by a little hill with pines surmounted,
Upon whose slant uprose a lordly mansion
Bright smiling over grove and lawn and garden.
A stately lady dwelt therein in comfort,
For 'twas a place where man might well feel easy.
Patrician she—she was no common creature—
Her fathers lived before the tyrant Tudors.
Great store of wealth had she—her smiling acres
Stretched far and wide o'er wood and hill and valley;
Yet she was good withal—a saintly matron,
Who strove to teach men how to duly honor
The Lord alway and rev'rence each his betters.
So morn and eve, when time was not too precious,
Or taken with affairs of more importance,
She gathered round her seat her poor domestics
And read for them the Book of Revelation,
Then sang a hymn, and prayed with earnest fervor:
And ever closed her prayer with this petition,
"O Lord, deal kindly with the common people!"

  The town was built upon a lower level,
And in it dwelt a host of toiling people;

ANSWERED PRAYER.

But many a cry went up for food and raiment,
For idle men fare ill, and they were idle;
And so it came to pass, their joint petition,
Their ceaseless cry, the lady's fervent praying,
Besieged the Throne till all the Court was weary,
And lo! the word went forth from God the Father,
"I even now will bless the toiling people."

  So from the boundless store the Lord had garnered
Fell to the earth a shower that well might gladden
The hearts of men whose food was always scanty,
And garments old and thin and past repairing;
But, best of all, the ample benediction
Fell fair within the park of that good lady:
The common herd would sure receive the blessing,
She thus could glory that her prayer was answered.
But life is ever full of contradiction;
The hills and vales re-echo with the jingle
Of loud protestings, void of sense or meaning,
And prayers that, answered, would displease the pleaders.

  The lady listless sat within the parlor,
And from her downy nest of purple velvet
Beheld the bounty of the Lord fall earthward.
In eager haste she called her trusty steward,
And bade him safely house whate'er had fallen,
Which thing he did; and much the lady marvelled
That man and maid alike should dare to murmur.
"They say, ''Tis mine—it came to me from heaven.'
The land is *mine*—who dares dispute my title!"
Then prayed she long, the Righteous God beseeching,
"Put honest hearts within the common people."

  Sun, moon and stars adore one great Creator;
The hills are His, and every shady valley;
Yet it hath come to pass, man hath ordained it,
God hath not room to bless His needy people.

A SERMON.

"Oh! Be ye contented!" he cried
   With uplifted hands and voice;
"That ye've raiment and victuals beside,
   Ye children of labor, rejoice.

"Your masters are lords of the soil,
   Their title ye cannot disprove;
They *sometimes* allow you to toil,
   Then serve and obey them with love.

"What though ye have hovels for homes,
   And your children go hungry and bare?
To murmur were base ingratitude,—
   Your Father hath placed you there.

"Soon, soon He will summon you hence.
   Oh, be wise and be patient till then,
For the Lord hath given the earth
   To a *few* of the children of men."

Thus he preached to the sons of toil,
   Thus he smote his Lord on the cheek;
For he ate the bread of the rich,
   And he spoke as they bade him speak.

So the toilers have bowed their necks
   To the yoke upon them laid,
Though their hearts cried out that the earth
   For all mankind was made.

But their day-star even now
   Beams 'cross the darkened way,
And heralds for those who toil
   The dawn of a brighter day.

THE LAND MONOPOLIST.

'Twas the eve of a chill November day,
As he sat at his desk in the gloaming gray,
And mused for awhile, ere the light was spent,
On his profits of mortgage and loan and rent.
He'd watched his pile grow night by night,
Though he had not toiled for the shekels bright,
So he softly sang as he stroked his chin,
"I gather them in, I gather them in.

"And why should I not, for I own the soil?
So my tenants must pay me for leave to toil:
By day and by night with the sweat of their brow
They have wrought for the harvest I'm reaping now;
And the cream of it all is my legal due—
If that suffice not the skimm'd milk too.
Their food may be poor and their raiment thin,
But my rents, my rents, I gather them in.

"I gather them in as the seasons go,
And the toilers sink lower, and still more low:
In spite of our progress they poorer grow,
In spite of our learning the less they know.
Soon the days of the years of their toil will be o'er,
Then they'll crawl to the yawning poor-house door,
Forsaken of friends and neglected by kin,—
But my rents, my rents, I gather them in."

TRUTH, UPHOLD AND GUIDE ME.

When life's way is as a stream
   Singing 'mong the peaceful meadows,
Stealing each bright sunbeam's gleam
   Through the greenwood's changeful shadows;
When no tempests toss or fret me,
And no frowning rocks beset me,
   Truth, uphold and guide me.

When by rocks I'm compassed round,
   And the sky is dark above me;
When the woods give back no sound
   That might teach me thou dost love me;
When my song is changed to weeping,
When the storm is o'er me sweeping,
   Truth, uphold and guide me.

As the stream must meet the sea,
   So must I death's icy billow;
When from narrowing rocks I'm free,
   Be thy mighty arm my pillow;
When I leave this world of sorrow,
For the vast unknown to-morrow,
   Truth, uphold and guide me.

NOT ALL.

Not all who preach are apostles,
  Nor a linnet is each if he sings;
Not all who bear titles are noble,
  Not all who sway sceptres are kings.

For a parrot may speak as a prophet,
  A devil may flutter white wings;
A siren may sing as a seraph,
  And revel in blood as she sings.

A lout may be viscount or marquis,
  A duke may be lacking in brains;
A prince be a coward or dastard,
  Polluted by vilest of stains.

The purple may cover a puppet
  Or tyrant supported by knaves,
Whose realm is the home of Oppression,
  His people a nation of slaves.

But he who is useful is noble,
  Tho' the soil to his garments may cling;
The foeman of Error is priestly,
  Who governs himself is a King.

THOU HAST NOT.

Hast thou counted the needles of all the pines
    That clothe all the mountains and hills?
Hast thou measured the tendrils of all the vines?
    Hast thou numbered the ripples of all the rills?
Hast thou counted the stars as they glitter above?
Then mayest thou know how a woman can love.

Since time began hast thou numbered his hours,
    Or the bursting buds of spring?
Hast thou bottled the perfume of all the flowers?
    Hast thou learned all the songs of the birds that sing?
Hast thou weighed all the valleys and counted their dust?
Then mayest thou know how a woman can trust.

Tho' slighted, despised, and betrayèd by man,
    And numbed in his race for gold,
They've been true till death since time began,
    They are ever young tho' as Eve they are old;
More precious than pearls or the gold's bright dust,
Or life, are a woman's love and trust.

NIGHT.

Between the earth's dank edge
   And fringe of gold and gray,
The sun a moment smiled
   Across the sodden plain,
Till all the east hills glowed,
   And e'en the dreary rain
Gave back his smile.
   The curtain fell and hid the day :
Apace the blackness grew
   Till e'en the twilight gray
Rolled back in dread before
   The songless, starless night
That brooded death-like
   Over vale, and lake, and bay,
Till all things that had been
   Seemed lost to life and light ;—
Fit emblem of the soul's
   Long restful, dreamless night !
Untroubled by a thought
   Of joy, or pain, or dread,
All reckless as the flowers
   Of Time's unwearying flight,
She sleeps her cleansing sleep
   The while she seemeth dead.
Unbroken thus her rest
   Till dawns her brighter day,
Or back to earth she soars
   To move a nobler clay.

LIFE.

Beside the brook th' unfolding violet frail,
   Ere its first noon, is crushed beneath the feet
   Of men ; or, scorched by fervent noontide heat,
Hath ceased to smile above the grassy vale.
The giant maple, as a warrior hale,
   Long reigning monarch of the autumn wood,
   His thousand scars bespeaking storms withstood,
Lies prone at last before a fiercer gale.
So, soon or late the life of man must fail.
   A hundred snows may whiten o'er his head,
Or but a day be his ; all one their tale :
   They came to earth, and paused a while, then fled.
All must bend low to Nature's kind decree ;
Each hath his day, but may not always be.

WHEN I FOLD MY HANDS.

When I fold my hands in my last long sleep,
   I would rest where the pine-trees sigh,
On some craggy steep that fronts the deep
   And frowns on the western sky;
Where billows' roar on that rock-bound shore,
   And the thunders that round it roll,
And the sea-bird's cry from the stormy sky,
   Might sing to my sleeping soul.

Or I'd rest far up on a mountain's side,
   On a ledge o'erhanging a lake,
Where the Douglas firs in that breezy air
   Their shadows across it shake;
Where mad torrents leap from steep to steep,
   To that dark lake's heaving breast,
And the sun's bright beams just glint in gleams
   As he sinks from the hills to rest.

THE SONG OF THE STORM KING.

When the day glides out through the western gates,
    And the angels of night draw nigh,
I love to list for their shadowy wings,
And the strains of song each phantom sings,
    As they come from the eastern sky—
    From the darkening eastern sky—
To meet by mountain and glade and brook,
And with the zephyrs, from Nature's book,
    Sing Earth's sweet lullaby.

From the twilight gray, through the darksome night,
    To the ruby dawn they sing;
And just as the chilly eastern breeze
Shakes the diamond dew from the sleeping trees,
    Their flight to the west they wing.
    Of the myriad songs they sing
Of the star-lit sky, of the dancing sea,
Or of love, there is none so sweet to me
    As this of the Tempest King.

He comes from his castle of coral and pearl,
    Far under the smiling sea,
Where the hurricane-blast in his cavern is found,
And the thunder in silence a season is bound,

Or mutters his prayer to be free.
  He only can make them free
When he leaps to the back of his nimbus black,
And above the meadows with bridle slack
  He scampers in boist'rous glee.

He darkens the sun while he roars at the earth,
  And laughs through his clattering rain.
His thunders re-echo from hill to hill,
His lightnings flash, and each freighted rill
  Leaps headlong down the plain.
  Man's puny strength is vain;
His mightiest works are crushed at a blow,—
One shining arrow will lay him low,
  To rebuild them never again.

He lashes the sea till her angry steeds
  Rear, champ and chafe and roar,
And, gathering strength from each strong last leap,
Forth rush from the breast of the surging deep
  Far up on the sloping shore.
  Oh, the sea doth roll and roar,
Till, like bubbles of air, the stately ships,
Engulfed by her yawning, greedy lips,
  Sink down to rise no more.

Or he comes from his home in the Frozen North,
  Where Aurora encircles his throne,
Where no man ever treadeth that desolate shore,
And no torrent forever again may roar,
  And no voice ever speak but his own.
  He comes in his might, alone,
And clothes all the lakes and green valleys below
With an armor of ice and a doublet of snow,
  From that silent crystal zone.

ON LIFE'S OCEAN.

SHORELESS and measureless, restless eternally,
  Ever the same to the left, to the right;
Darkness in front of us, uplooming dismally,
  Darkness behind as the blackness of night!

Here it is calm as a pool in the prairie-land,
  There it is white in its rage with a reef;
Here it is bright as a phantom of fairy-land,
  There it is dark as the gloom-land of Grief.

Now it is slow, and again it is currentless,
  Then it is swift as the Ottawa's tide;
Now not a breeze bellies sails that hang motionless,
  Then shrieks a gale that no sailor may ride.

Fierce though the storms that anon bellow over it,
  Frail are the vessels that over it glide;
Tossed like its spray are the shallops that cover it,
  Toys of its tempests, its calms and its tides.

Oft must they drive through the mist that is shrouding
    them,
    Straight on the rocks where no warning bell tolls;
Oft must they sail where a beacon gleams, crowding them
    On to the treacherous sands of its shoals.

They who are weak labor wearily, wearily,
    Helplessly buffeted, glad to be gone;
Sinking at nightfall 'mid winds sighing drearily,
    Never once missed, while the billows roll on.

Many a seaman wrecks wilfully, wilfully—
    So say the prudent whom Fortune has cheered;
They see where he foundered, and steer from it skilfully,
    But know not the breakers his strong arm had cleared.

Sometimes one sinks, and some sigh for him mournfully,
    Sad he no longer their sea-mate may be;
But what of the words they had uttered so scornfully
    When half of his vessel was under the sea?

Better a cheer when the white waves were tossing him;
    Better a light when the gloom gathered round;
Better a line when the current was crossing him,
    Than cannon to boom when his keel is aground.

Shoreless and measureless, restless eternally,
    We are the foam of thy dark billow's crest;
Borne from its mane on the wind moaning dismally,—
    Whither? What matter, if only to rest?

THE AWAKENING.

Every vale and hill
  Deep in slumber lay;
Hushed was every rill,
  All the wood was gray.
But the purple dawn
  Trembles in the sky;
Nature's night is o'er,
  Day is drawing nigh.
Northward from the isles
  Where the orange blooms,
Where palmettos tall
  Rear their nodding plumes
Where the zephyrs kiss
  Ever-vernal trees,
Where no breath of Thule
  Smiteth birds or bees,
Lightly tripped a youth
  Through the valleys deep,
Nature to arouse
  From her dreamless sleep.
Softly as the sun
  Sinks into the sea,

THE AWAKENING.

Gently as the vine
   Twines the stalwart tree,
By her couch he trod
   'Mong the shadows deep,
By his balmy kiss
   Wooed her from her sleep.
Ruddy blushed the twain
   At their wanton play,
Till her snowy robes
   Rolled in mist away.
She behind her veil,
   Wrought of silver sheen,
Smiling through her tears,
   Donned her garb of green.
So the youth awoke,
   Her who slept so long,
Filling all her soul
   With unceasing song.

TO CANADA.

LAND of the Maple and Fir,
Mighty domain of the West,
Kissed by three oceans at once,
Thou art the home of my youth,
Thou art the land that I love !
    Rich are thy prairies, and fair
The slopes where thy peach-orchards blush ;
Treasures of silver and gold,
Treasures of iron and coal,
Treasures of timber and corn,
Lie at the feet of thy sons.
Then whence is the spectre Want
That with pitiless, hungry eyes,
And merciless fingers and gaunt,
Follows thy children who toil ?
    Love thee ? Ay, love thee I do,
Else, like the tinklers in verse,
I had covered thee over with lies.
Have I not played in thy dells,
Dreamed by thy murmuring rills,
Lulled by the moan of thy pines ?
Now, when no longer a child,
I weep that the sons thou hast borne

Tarnish thy fame with their deeds;
Weep that our law-givers clutch,
As babes clutch at bubbles of air,
At ribbons with pins for their coats,
Then ape all the follies, and worse,
Of their grandsires' grandsires gone;
Weep o'er the discord and din
That moan from the East to the West,
Over thy mountains and plains,
Like the wail of a gathering storm
That to-morrow in fury may burst
And flood thee in blood and in tears!
Patriot, Plunderer, Fraud,
All sound the same in our ears.
Position, Property, Pelf,
Are jewels that dazzle the eye,
Till Honesty, Honor and Truth
Are baubles for children and fools,
And men, the creators of things,
Are slaves to the things they have made.
E'en the Pulpit has jostled the Pew,
To fall at the feet of the calf.

    Love thee? Ay, love thee and mourn
That the crown of thy glory is dross.
Tinsel and bunting and smoke
Are not of greatness the pledge.
When thy sons and thy daughters are free,
Free from the thraldom of gold,
Free from the wars of their creeds,
Free from the terror of want;
Free in the freedom of Love,
Honesty, Honor and Truth,
Then shalt thou truly be great,
O Land of the Maple and Fir!

IT MIGHT HAVE BEEN.

OFT sadly say we, "Thus and thus it might have been,"
   While, standing dazed with weary hands and listless,
With streaming eyes, and hearts all crushed and bleeding,
We watch our god, Ambition, fast receding
   Before the hands unseen, unknown, resistless,
That thrust him from the shrine our hands had builded,
And crushed the fairy fane our fancy gilded.
      Oh, woeful, woeful scene!

We scan the wreck and sigh, "Oh, woeful, woeful scene!"
   Till sunlight dies, dark shadows only leaving;
Fair flowers fade beside the way we're treading;
We drown their life in salt tears we are shedding,
   And point each thorn with vain and selfish grieving.
We mourn that aught our perfect plan should alter;
We loathe our lot, in childish accents falter—
      "It might, it might have been!"

As outbound ships where not a beacon star is seen,
   Or through a cloud that, weary of its soaring,
Has sunk to rest upon the billows heaving,
The seen and unseen, all behind us leaving,

IT MIGHT HAVE BEEN.

We drift adown life's current onward pouring,
But are not tossed by every gale that bloweth:
The log we bear is not a log that showeth
    All ills that might have been.

'Twere well to smile, nor moan "Oh, woeful, woeful scene!"
    When vane and tow'r and painted window crumble.
The past is gone! Why sadness from her borrow?
If foiled to-day, we'll victors be to-morrow,
    Or learn from failure to be wise and humble.
'Twere better far our days to spend in trying,
Though worsted always, than in idly sighing,
    "It might, it might have been!"

LIFE.

Life is not measured by the days we number;
  Our threescore years and ten may prove a breath;
To eat and drink and fold the hands in slumber
  Is but a living death.

His life is long who, faithful to his calling,
  Hath made the most of all his precious hours;
Though few his days, his deeds, like dewdrops falling,
  Have strewed his path with flowers.

Oh, then be wise. Waste not thy time in waiting;
  Be up and act before thy chance be past;
With golden deeds thy fleeting moments freighting
  As though each were thy last.

TO GRANDMA.

To-night alone and sad I sit
   And ponder Mem'ry's pages o'er,
Till Absence makes each pictured tale
   More dear than it had been before;
Tho' hills uploom and plains outspread,
   And brawling torrents roll between,
In thought I leave this sounding shore,
   To seek each well-remembered scene.

Each fond familiar face returns
   As thro' the sunny house I move;
Again my failing heart is cheered
   By warm, unbought, unselfish love.
I see thee move from place to place,
   To touch some dim and clouded eye,
Some fevered, throbbing brow to cool,
   The tear of dark Despair to dry.

As slow I turn sweet Mem'ry's page,
   In characters of gold I see
A thousand words of tender cheer,
   A thousand deeds of love to me:

TO GRANDMA.

Full oft when chill Dejection's hand
   Pressed heavy on this heart of mine,
A voice would speak of brighter days,
   And, truest friend, that voice was thine.

The future may be clouded yet,
   The present may not all be glad ;
The past, a joyous summer's dream,
   Returns to cheer me when I'm sad.
Whate'er betide, afar or near,
   In weal or woe, on land or sea,
My grateful heart will beat her thanks
   For all thy tender care for me.

THE FROST.

Out of the depths of the Autumn sky,
  Into the hearts of the sleeping flow'rs,
  Speedeth the Frost in the drear, dark hours,
And the wild winds wail that the fair ones die.

Thro' the Autumn's gray and the blue of Spring,
  There hasteth an Angel with icy breath:
  His heart throbs not, and we name him Death,
For a fair one falls if he stay his wing.

And that soundless wing full oft he stays
  While he lays some form that we cherish low,
  Nor recks that our blinding tears fast flow,
That our flow'ret fades in the Spring of his days.

And the garlands sweet that Ambition wreathes,
  So fair in the flush of Morning bright,
  Are wet with the tears of sad, cold Night,
For their beauty fades where the keen Frost breathes.

THE FROST.

Is the year then lost if the Frost doth fall?
   Is the great Sun quenched by the Autumn's rain?
   If we love and lose is Love then vain?
Shall the fiend Despair our hearts enthrall?

If our garlands fade we will fairer weave,
   Nor weep that their gloom had pass'd away;
   If the Sun is hid by the clouds all day
We will watch for his smile in the peaceful eve.

Tho' no heart respond we will love the more;
   For Love is God—we will teach men so,
   Till poor or rich each soul shall know,
As a loveless life no life is so poor.

Then the Frost may stoop on his soundless wing,
   But the sky tho' dark shall again be bright,
   For Hope, on pinions of deathless Light,
Still hymns to our hearts of eternal Spring.

NOVEMBER.

Loud, loud the wild wind of November is wailing,
    Down from the hill-lands, thro' the wild gorges,
Out o'er the sodden sands, thro' shattered vines trailing,
    Over the leaping Lake's white-crested surges.

Shrill sings the water-wraith, deep roar the billows,
    Far up the sloping shore fierce chargers prancing;
Stand with uncovered heads grim ancient willows,
    Waving their wrinkled arms like wizards dancing.

Far away over me dark clouds are wallowing,
    Like serried warriors meeting and battling;
Over the swaying pines their thunder is bellowing,
    Down on the yellow leaves sharp hail is rattling.

Yest're'en among the ferns dreamily rhyming,
    Now see yon brawling brook wildly tumultuous,
Bright when the sky was bright, sweet carols chiming,
    Now as its neighbors are, hoarse and tempestuous.

NOVEMBER.

Bare are the daisy-banks, where are the flowers?
  Under the Autumn leaves dreamlessly sleeping;
Lull'd by the parting songs of sweet Summer's bowers,
  Now wilder melody over them sweeping.

Out o'er the wat'ry waste lone gulls are calling:
  Now with the storm they go, now tempests breasting;
Yet all is well, I hear like music falling,
  "This is not Death but Rest, weary Life resting."

What tho' in glade and glen slumber the flowers!
  Glad are November's songs—he knows no dirges;
What tho' no oriole calls from the bowers!
  Even and morn are mine, Songs of the Surges.

ON THE SHORE I STOOD AT EVEN.

On the shore I stood at even,
Where the wild winds whirled around me,
From the hollows, leaves of Autumn,
    Sere and dry;
And the great Lake lay before me,
Like a restless giant cradled,
With his long white fingers clutching
At the pinions, stooping pinions
    Of the Sky.

Lower drooped those wings, and lower,
As of angel foster-mother
O'er a loved one fondly bending
    In the Night;
And the glad Lake roll'd and revell'd,
And his laugh grew loud and louder,
As he gaily toss'd toward her,
From his bosom, foamy feathers
    Soft and white.

Lo! the Spirit of Polaris
Had that mighty cradle girdled
With a wreath of rarest crystal
    From his throne;
And the Sea-sprites sang in chorus,
To the wingèd Tempest's music,
Till my world of care had vanished,
And I knew no soul had gladness
    Like my own.

Night perennial gathers o'er me,
And I name it Spring or Autumn
As my feet disperse the hoar-frost
    Or the dew;
Still the Zephyrs softly kiss me,
And the Roses breathe upon me,
But sweet Summer's slumb'rous sonnets
Reach me but in dreamy echoes
    From the blue.

So I love the Storm that thunders
Thro' the naked nodding Forest,
Beating measures with the billows
    Wild and white;
For my life was ever stormy,
And my soul doth chafe within me
Like a scion of the Tempest,
That would soar beyond the confines
    Of the Night.

A CHRISTMAS SONG.

Oh, ring, oh, ring, oh, ring,
    Your silver bells with gladness!
Oh, sing, oh, sing, oh, sing,
    And banish care and sadness!
Come crown with cheer the hoary year,
    Come bury Grief and Fretting,
For once again e'en selfish men
    Love giving more than getting.

Oh, gladsome, gladsome Morn,
    Excelling ev'ry other,
When Love anew is born
    And man to man is brother:
When blinding Self nor sordid Pelf
    Are deem'd Life's fairest treasures,
When he who shares a brother's cares
    Doth taste of rarest pleasures!

'Tis goodly, bright and fair,
    This gem in baser setting,
But oh! to-morrow's air
    Will ring with praise of Getting;
Then pray that we soon, soon may see,
    That Sunrise, rich and golden,
When all the earth at second birth,
    Shall sing that anthem olden.

THOU LORD SEEST ME.

I'm glad Thou, Father, seest all the way
   That I must tread before the sun shall set;
I'm glad Thou knowest all the fleeting day,
   And ev'ry ill my waiting soul doth fret.

I'm glad Thou, Father, lovest well to hear
   The voice that unto man is mean or mute;
I'm glad Thou seest where Love's light is clear,
   Tho' erring man may motive base impute.

I'm glad Thou markest from thy dwelling-place
   Each trivial act of love, each tender word;
I'm glad no mists of doubt can hide my face
   From Thee, O Gracious Father, Righteous Lord.

I'm glad Thou seest ev'ry slip and fall
   Upon this hilly, thorny, rugged path;
I'm glad Thou know'st well the why of all,
   And judgest them in love and not in wrath.

O Father, I am glad Thou seest me,
   From morn to eve, in calm and tempest wild;
Do Thou but lead, I'll gladly follow Thee,
   For Thou dost love full well Thy wand'ring child.

THE OLD YEAR AND THE NEW.

FAR in the North-land the virgin Aurora
　Rustled her curtain, soft-woven in light;
Deep within deep bosom'd many an ember,
Glow-worms resplendent of icy December,
　Lighting the noontide of night.

Lightly the East-wind trod where the Snow-sprite
　Slumber'd awhile in the woodland below;
The Rill thro' the meadow crept counting his pebbles,
And sang 'neath his breath in his soft silv'ry trebles,
　"Pansies sleep under the snow."

Out of the dell where the shadows had gather'd,
　Shadowy wayfarers glided that night:
Weary and feeble was one, heavy-laden,
Strong was the other and fair as a maiden;
　Fair was their armor and white.

THE OLD YEAR AND THE NEW.

"Oh!" sigh'd the Sage as they journey'd together,
  "Gladly I'll hence with my burden to-night:
Into the blue with my folly and madness,
Heart-aches and sighings, my tears and my sadness,
  Hatred and railing and spite.

Hopes have I gather'd as maids gather roses;
  Shrivell'd their form in the red Autumn's glow;
Wanton the winds of my garlands bereft me,
They and the reaper have ruthlessly left me
  Nothing but ashes of snow."

Then from the hill-top he rose with his sighing,
  Rose with his heart-aches, his railing, his tears,
Rose till a gem in Night's diadem gleaming,
Down on the snowy Earth lovingly beaming,
  Brightest of sons of the years.

"Whither away?" of the youth then I queried,
  "What dost *thou* carry? Whence dost *thou* come?"
Softly the muffled Rill there in the meadow
Trill'd me this answer back out of the shadow,
  "He till to-morrow is dumb."

LIFE'S BATTLE-FIELD.

I stood upon the wide, wide tented field;
   I heard the clarion's clanging near and far;
I saw the blazé of banner, glare of shield;
   I felt the plunging tide of ruthless War.

I saw the serried hosts that forth and back
   Were march'd and counter-march'd across the plain;
I saw the wasting flame, the ruins black;
   I saw the tears that fell above the slain.

I saw the lonely vigils of the Night
   That faithful pickets kept while others slept:
Full many a gallant unrecorded fight
   Before some pass one, single-handed, kept.

Anon a warrior, spurred and belted, came,
   Whose breast was hid 'neath blazen-jewell'd stars:
His were the laurels, his the loud acclaim,
   While they who follow'd bore but wounds and scars.

He glowed a goodly Sun, but lo! the light
   Was but a spark that he might call his own;
For round him whirled full many a satellite
   That fed the flame that burned before his throne.

Pale Famine, stalking, filled with nameless dread
   The stoutest hearts, and nerveless left strong arms;
Feet faltered that from foe had never fled,
   Eyes dimmed that ne'er had dimmed at War's alarms.

Tho' many a tent grew still and dark and cold,
   Time-serving minions sped on hurrying feet,
On silver salvers bearing pearls and gold
   To those whose store had ever been complete.

Forced marches, bivouacs, unremitting strife,
   Frost, famine, battle, watches drear and lone,—
Some bore them all nor murmured; yet in life
   They asked for bread, their answer now a stone.

And far and near were mounds that covered those
   Whose hands had never warred for place or prize,
Yet here may pause alike their friends and foes,
   And read their date in costly sculptured lies.

O Prince of Peace! Cut short this wasting strife,
   Call order from this chaos by Thy will;
Bid right be might, command that love be life,
   Lord, o'er this tented field speak "Peace, be still."

A VISION OF HELL.

Upon an Isle that seemed a garden fair,
By hidden cords dependent 'twixt two seas
Of rarest blue, I stood and watched the sun,
A ship of golden flame, glide thro' the Gates,
Where, in a radiant flood of regal glory,
      Those oceans blent their billows.

A gentle breeze swept o'er the nether sea,
And, lo! adown the wake of that fair ship
Unnumbered glowing rubies burned to show
Where it had passed; while eastward from the shore
The glacier slopes of snow-crowned crags gave back
Its parting smile. The dark'ning cliffs along
The margin of the main beheld their face,—
With ev'ry strange fantastic line that Time
And Ocean with unwearying, briny hand,
Had written there in play or frenzied passion,
      Within the shadowed waters.

A VISION OF HELL.

And o'er the gath'ring gloom and waning light,
And thro' the trees there swept soft slumb'rous strains
As of the vesper hymn the Night-wind sings,
With murm'ring rills, where Fairy Ferns bend low
And tell their beads by Venus' constant lamp.
Lo! in a woodland dell hard by the sea
I saw an altar reared, and round it stood
Strong men and goodly women, and they sang;
And standing on the beach the Night-wind bore
The voice of all their gladness to my ear.
"No fetter forged by father binds the son;
No son shall pay the debt his father ought;
I live where Freedom reigns, and free I live
Unto myself; unto myself I die."
While thus they sang the Night soar'd down upon me
  And by the sea I slumbered.

The dank, dark Night went down into the sea,
And o'er the hills the Sun, in hot pursuit,
Shot crimson arrows at him as he went;
Then Sleep with gentle hands undid the bands
With which the day before she bound my limbs,
Then left me and I stood upon my feet.
The boundless sea, the everlasting hills,
The cliffs, the dell, the music of the rills,
Were all as fair as when I fell asleep;
But where the altar was a fire now blazed,
And round it danced a naked savage tribe.
Each jostled each to clutch with bloody hands
At half-broiled fragments of a brother's form,
And sang the while their war-song shrill and wild,—
A song no man of any other land
Save this could sing, save this could understand.
My heart grew sick, my limbs support denying,
  And once again I slumbered.

Again the night had fled before the day,
And, like an artist's canvas fair outspread,
The landscape, sea, and sky around me lay.
The rills, kissed into smiling by the sun,
Sang back their love from many a grassy glen,
And ev'ry breath of ev'ry breeze that passed
Was heavy freighted with the roses' sigh.
No answ'ring voice was there in all the land—
No robin's note, no love-lorn maiden's lay,
No gleeful laugh of children by the brook,
No plowman's cheery call across the glebe,
No gentle mother's soothing lullaby;
For all things animate had ceased to be.
No creature moved save loathsome, shapeless things
That squirmed within the slimy depths unfathomed,
    Of dim plague-haunted marshes.

NORMA.

Gently down a verdant valley,
Down a rich and fertile valley,
Flanked by many a sloping meadow,
Here and there with copses dotted,
Shading homes of thrifty yeomen,
Glides a limpid, murm'ring streamlet.
All day long it is a mirror,
Smiling back at smiling nature,
And a band of burnished silver
When the moon is in the zenith.
Just below a bridge of timber,
Flung across by sturdy rustics,
Lo! it broadens to a lakelet,
To a pool of liquid crystal,
Motionless, save when the breezes
Ruffle all its shining bosom,
And its tiny plashing ripples
Babble on their beach of pebbles—
Babble on the pebbled border
Of an emerald lawn of velvet

Slanting from the ivied cottage
Of the stalwart James Fitz Maurice,
Father of the lovely Norma.

Here the summer of her childhood
Sped in blissful freedom onward,
As she grew an agile maiden,
Supple as a wand of willow,
Blithe as roe in virgin forest,
Fiercer than the fierce tornado
When her restless soul was angered.
As the timid fawn is gentle,
So was she to those who knew her.
She had wandered through the woodland
When the trees sang in the morning,
Heard the hymn they sang at twilight.
All the rills in all the valleys
Were her playmates and companions;
And she loved them, for they taught her
Of the great All-wise Creator.
And she read the book of Nature,
Read the golden Revelation,
Saw in all its shining pages
Love unbounded, love unchanging.
Every hill and vale and river,
Every star and cloud and blossom,
Breathed the love of God the Giver;
And the tempest, and the thunder
Only sang in accents louder,
"God is Love to all His creatures."
So she learned ere twenty summers
Of her life were past recalling,
Learned to see all men as brothers,
Children of one common Father.

To the bosom of the mountains,
To the valley of the Fraser,
Where the pine and Douglas fir-tree
Make his waters black at noon-day;
Where the axe of brawny woodman,
And the saw-mills, merry humming,
Fill the vale with ceaseless music
That re-echoes in the mountains,
Norma from the East did journey,
Took a journey o'er the prairies
To her sister's far-off dwelling.
When the blue was farthest upward,
And the lakes seemed clearest, deepest,
And the birds sang loudest, sweetest,
And the rose was blooming, went she.
Days flew by till weeks were numbered
While she rambled o'er the mountains,
Or along the rushing river,
Through the darkness of the forest,
Wandered with her dog and rifle.
Far adown the stream one morning
Rode she to a snow-capped mountain
That she had not yet ascended;
In a grassy dell dismounted,
Tied her bronco to a sapling,
While from cliff to crag she clambered
That she might behold the Ocean,
Might behold the broad Pacific,
As it gamboled in the sunshine.
All day long she roamed the mountain,
Heeding not the level sunbeams,
Till the sun was nearly hidden;
Then descending for her pony,
Found the dell in deepest shadow,

Found the broken hempen halter,
But no saddled bronco found she.
All alone among the mountains
Stood she musing for a moment
On the way that lay before her.
She was far from human dwelling;
Lay her sister's home more distant;
And the path that she must traverse
Was the rugged trail of miners,
Lonely in the ghostly moonlight.
Vain the task to seek her pony,
For she could not trace his foot-prints;
So alone in all the silence
She must walk to yonder village.
Firmly as on city pavement,
Blithely as it were but pastime,
Stepped she from the shaded valley,
Stepped she forth upon her journey.
Over hills, through gloomy valleys,
Crossing streams on fallen timbers,
Past the still lake's checkered waters,
She completed half the distance,
When upon a sandy hillock,
Motionless as if of marble
Tow'ring dark against the heavens
In the way that she was treading,
Stood a stalwart horse and rider.
Ere she reached the hillock summit
Had her eagle eye discovered
That the bronzed and bearded horseman
Was the rancher, Gerald Gordon.
He, while riding o'er the meadows,
Found the pony idly feeding.
Wondering greatly as he caught it

What mishap had her befallen,
He had paused upon the hilltop
Much perplexed and undecided
What to do to find the maiden.
So he sat, when just behind him
Norma, laughing, loudly hailed him:
"Stand, I say, and prithee tell me
What you do here with my bronco?
Seven long miles I've walked, or over,
Just to find you speculating
On the price of stolen ponies."
Then unto the truant turning,
"Oh, impatient Tuscarora,
Was the waiting over weary?
Hadst for me so small affection
That thou needs must break thy tether,
And forsake the friend that feeds thee?"
While she thus her horse was chiding
She the saddle girth did tighten,
And before the 'stonished Gerald
Could collect his scattered senses,
She was seated in the saddle,
Ready for the scamper homeward.
As they galloped gaily onward
She recounted all her rambles,
All her wand'rings on the mountain,
Told him all the day's adventures,
Till he blessed the wayward pony;
For his heart grew warm within him
As they journeyed in the moonlight.

So July gave place to August,
(Low the harvest-moon was waning,)
And the day for her returning

To that far-off Eastern valley
Nearer grew and ever nearer.
Gerald Gordon loved her fondly,
With a love both strong and tender,
And she loved him for his manhood,
Loved him for his dauntless courage,
Prized him for his soul of honor;
But she had not thought on marriage,
Never deemed that she might wed him.
'Twas a night when angels wonder
At the earth's transcendent beauty,
Fold their wings and sadly ponder
On the loveless lives of mortals.
From the bosom of the forest
Came the zephyrs' dreamy humming,
Floating o'er the dappled water
Of a lake whose rolling ripples
Sang in slumb'rous silvery trebles
All along its grassy margin;
And the thousand constellations
Sang around the Moon's pavilion.
Scarce a furlong from the water
Rose a hill abrupt and rugged,
Clad with firs and strewn with boulders.
All between the lake and mountain
Was a level, smooth and grassy:
This the village park and garden,
Play-ground of the village children,
Trysting-place of happy lovers.
Here it was that Norma daily
Loved to linger in the gloaming,
Loved to loiter in the moonlight;
Here it was that Gerald found her.

Gently to and fro they wandered.
Neither spoke for many moments,
For the pine-trees, breathing incense,
And the silence, soft and peaceful,
Seemed as of a sacred cloister;
While their souls were upward lifted
Far beyond the spangled heavens.
But at last he softly murmured,
"Norma, all my heart I give thee;
All I am or ever shall be,
All I have or ever shall have,
Lay I at thy feet as tribute.
Never wooed I other maiden.
Thou art of my life the sunshine;
Well thou knowest that I love thee,
Yet thy face hast not betrayed thee.
Norma, tell me, dost thou love me?
Norma, wilt thou some day wed me?"
Then he paused and gazed upon her,
Long in silence gazed upon her,
Mutely for an answer pleading;
But she walked as all unconscious
That he even walked beside her.
But at last as one arousing
From a dread or troubled vision,
Raised her eyes and spoke she to him:
"Gerald, thou dost much distress me.
All the summers I have numbered
Well thou knowest are not twenty;
All my life is yet before me.
I am but a wayward maiden,
But a child, too young for wedlock;
And the love that now I bear thee—

For I truly love thee fondly—
Is the love as of a sister.
And thou dost not understand me:
Thou hast seen of all my nature
Nothing save the gentle sunshine;
Of the roaring, angry tempest,
That would crush the friend most tender,
Thou hast heard no distant murmur.
Thou shalt be to me a brother;
On my life, I dare not wed thee."

Long and earnestly he pleaded,
For he was an ardent lover;
But the loyal heart of woman
Strong within her grew and stronger:
She her hand would give to no man
If her heart might not go with it.
So she told him; but he loved her
With a love more strong and fervent.
Then they homeward turned their footsteps,
For the early moon was setting.
As they sought the hillside cottage
Both their hearts were bowed and heavy,
Knowing they must part to-morrow;
So they talked of happy moments
Gone adown Time's backward current,
And as mortals scan the future
Read the lives that lay before them,
Till they reached the cottage parlor;
Then he needs again must hear her
Sing, and so with heart aweary
Sang she of another parting.

"FAREWELL."

Farewell, farewell, forever more, farewell!
We met, we lived our day of love, we part;
What though the breast in bitter anguish swell,
What matter though it crush and numb the heart,
How much 'twill bear before it cease to beat!
What longing that the tongue may never tell!
Thro' hope deferred it hopes in patience sweet,
Only at last to hear the winds repeat,
    "Farewell, farewell!"
Farewell, dear heart! I would no storm or cloud
May ever gather o'er thy onward path;
I would in grief thy soul may ne'er be bowed,
Till Death himself is overcome by death.
While Time shall last thy mem'ry I'll retain;
Short-lived thy joy, tho' I have loved thee well;
My portion here the longing, yearning pain,
Life's soonest learned, most often heard refrain,
    Farewell, farewell.

    As he slowly rose to leave her,
    Once again for hope he pleaded,
    Then upon the threshold parted
    While the heart of each re-echoed,
    "Fondest heart, farewell, farewell!"

    Summer smiling flitted southward,
    While the lusty reaper, Autumn,
    Wreathed the hills with gold and crimson.
    Filled he all the vales with vapor,
    Shining in the sun of morning,
    Till the pine-woods seemed as islands

Springing from a sea of silver.
Shook he from the beech and hazel
Winter food for mouse and squirrel;
Then he breathed upon the flowers,
On the golden-rod and aster,—
All the rest had gone before them,
All the sweetest and the fairest,
While in pride of strength they flaunted
Till the blighting breath of Autumn
Fell upon them, and they perished,
Perished from the wood forever.
When the Spring shall burst the fetters
That have bound the streams in silence,
Every hill and dell shall revel
In the smile of other blossoms;
But the gems that fell last Autumn
Low shall lie as Autumn laid them.
Such the life of all things living,
Man is even as the flowers.

To the cottage by the lakeside,
To the cottage clad with ivy,
Norma had returned with Autumn,
Bearing with her joy and sunshine.
Ere the blast of chill November
Stripped the trees of all their glory,
Came there to the home of Norma
Donald Graham from the city.
He had played with her in childhood,
As a growing youth had loved her;
Now when crowned with sturdy manhood
Came he from his home to woo her.
In his heart he loved her truly,
And he thought to quickly win her,

For her father and her mother
Looked upon him and they prized him—
Prized him for his gold and silver,
Prized him for his proud position.
So they gave him words of counsel,
And they daily talked with Norma:
Told her of the ease and honor
She might have if she would wed him.
In him saw she but the playmate,
But the generous-hearted school-boy,
She had loved in early childhood,
And the heart yearned not toward him;
So she answered all their counsel,
Answered all her lover's pleadings,
With a short but earnest answer,
She should wed him when she loved him.
Then they told her love would ripen
If she were but wedded duly;
But she valued true affection
Far above all wealth and honor,
And her parents and her lover
Knew her will might not be bended.
So with this uncertain answer,
"I will wed thee when I love thee,"
He betook him to the city,
There to wait the maiden's pleasure.

Lo! the North King, like a giant,
Loosened from his crystal castle,
Roared across the open prairie,
Roared across Superior's waters.
Cold his breath and cold his fingers,
And his very heart was frozen;
Where he trod the earth grew rigid.

'Twixt the twilight and the dawning
Stood he in that Eastern valley,
Touched the lips of all the streamlets,
Sealed them till each muffled murmur,
Till their very soul of music,
Silent grew and died within them.
O'er the lake his wand of magic
Waved till on its shining surface
Grew a smooth transparent causeway.
Then his mighty wings he fluttered,
Sifting tiny plumes of crystal
Over hill and wood and meadow.
When the tardy sun awakened,
Shot his level arrows forward,
Lo! the fir-tree and the cedar,
Veiled as brides of blust'ring Winter,
Stood with folded arms to greet him;
And the oak-tree and the maple,
And the beech, and birch, and larch-tree,
All had donned another glory,
For a sheen of countless diamonds
Sparkled in the early sunrise.
So is Nature ever constant,
Ever kind and full of beauty,
Never killed by frosty winter,
Only robed in other raiment;
For the hills and dells re-echo
With the gleeful song of coasters,
With the joyous shouts of skaters,
And the sleigh-bells' merry chiming.

Soft lights quivered, dreamy music
Floated from a hidden alcove,
Floated from the gilded ball-room

Where had gathered youth and beauty.
Many a fair and stately lady,
Many a bright-eyed lovely maiden,
Blushed when gallant praised her beauty;
But the rose of all that garland
Was the dark-eyed queenly Norma;
No one in the waltz so graceful.
Yet she soon of dancing wearied,
Stealing to a spacious window
Where behind its ample curtains
She might sit and muse a season.
Oscar missed her from the dancers;
Here it was he sought and found her.
Neither e'er had seen the other
Till that night, yet few the moments
Ere they talked as friends long-knitted.
Soon they left the shadowed window,
Joined again the merry dancers;
But a richer, sweeter music
Raised their souls to higher levels:
Each had found a kindred spirit.
Soon approached the hour of parting
With its farewell's hollow tinkle,
But their eyes met eyes that answered,
And they knew they were not strangers:
Norma knew she loved, and Oscar,
Pledged to wed another maiden,
Loved her as he loved no other.
So they parted on that morning;
And as barks apart they drifted,
Sailed adown Time's changeful current,
Ne'er again to meet till nightfall;
Then a moment spoke each other,
And upon the great to-morrow

Anchored side by side in harbor.
True hearts break not over crosses
That no man may thwart or hinder.

Giant Spring came softly treading,
Pierced the icy heart of Winter;
Then the smiling youthful victor
Kissed the lips of smiling Nature,
To arouse her from her slumber.
Sunny May spread forth her verdure,
From afar her songsters wooing,
Till the woods rang with the music
Of their free and joyous chorus.
Then it was the rancher Gerald
Journeyed o'er the prairies eastward,
Sought and found his lost love, Norma.
Once again his cause he pleaded,
Told her she would learn to love him;
So it was at last she yielded.
When the first red rose was blushing
Gerald led her to the altar;
Then rejoicing took her with him
To his home among the mountains.
Donald Graham's heart was stricken.
Many months he nursed his sorrow,
Deeming none might ever heal it;
But one day he met a maiden
Full of life and youth and beauty.
Sweetly did she smile upon him,
And her every word was music
Soothing all his wounded spirit.
As the weeks went by he loved her
And she all his love requited,
So his broken heart she mended
When his name she took upon her.

Peaceful years flew swiftly over
Gerald's home among the mountains;
Stronger grew his love for Norma
And her love grew yet more tender,
Till one day a tiny maiden
Came to seal their bond of union,
Came to bless the life of Norma.

But a cloud, a hand-breadth over,
Gathering on her clear horizon,
Grew till all her sun was hidden,
Grew till all her sky was darkened.
Laura Gray had once loved Gerald
With a fierce, unbridled passion,
But he looked not kindly on her;
So as months and years sped onward
Love was changed to bitter hatred,
And her mind was ever burdened
With a longing for his ruin.
She might slay him, but she would not—
That were fit revenge for children;
She should smite the one he loved most,
Pierce him through his best affections.
So with studied art she poisoned
Many a mind that deemed her truthful,
Till the simple, unreflecting,
Looked askance at patient Norma.
Many a friend who lately loved her
Listened to the voice of slander,
But the noble-minded Gerald
Doubted not her love or virtue.
Still his heart was sorely wounded
When he saw his wife suspected.
By the river in the twilight

Norma walked alone one even.
Ev'ry breeze had hushed its whisper,
Ev'ry bird had ceased its singing;
Darksome clouds o'erspread the heavens,
And the thunder in the mountains
Told her of a storm approaching.
She had turned toward her cottage,
Distant half a league or under,
When she met her fair defamer.
Face to face they stood a moment,
Then the self-convicted Laura
Fell upon the earth in terror,
Craving mercy of her victim.
Norma stood in triumph o'er her,
Stood the very soul of Vengeance.
Only one short sentence spake she,
"Viper, had my husband doubted
I would slay thee where thou liest,"
Then she passed into the darkness.
Burst the storm in all its fury
O'er the fainting form of Laura,
And the cold rain beating o'er her
Roused her from her death-like stupor.
Slowly turned she from the village,
For her home was up the river.
From behind a moss-grown boulder,
Close beside her, to the pathway
Strode a miner, Martin Dumont,
Laura's once rejected lover;
And he hoarsely whispered to her,
"Years ago I loved thee truly,
And it seemed thou e'en didst love me,
But when thou hadst heard me woo thee,
And my love for thee had proven,

Then with scorn and loud derision,
Bade me woo some other maiden.
Now I've seen thy spirit humbled.
All the years of pain and longing
Now are gone, and all forgiven,
And I come again thy suitor;
Laura, Laura, wilt thou wed me?"
Maddened that he saw her terror,
Sprang she from his side and answered,
"Once I scorned thee, still I scorn thee,
And to-night I more despise thee.
When asked I for thy forgiveness?
Prate to one who loves to listen!
I would go, for I am weary;
Save thy love for gentle maidens—
To revenge my soul is wedded."
Then he whispered still more hoarsely,
"Well I know fair Norma's hatred
And the cause you gave her for it.
If she killed you who would marvel?
If they found you in the river
Stiff and stark to-morrow morning,
Who would say she had not killed you?
Woman, say that thou wilt wed me,
Or I swear by all things living
You shall die as I have told you."
Strove she once again to 'scape him,
But he quickly stood before her;
Through and through the heart he smote her;
Shrieked she one wild shriek of anguish,
Fell a lifeless corpse before him.
Then he raised the prostrate body,
Bore it to the river margin,
Where with all his strength he hurled it

Far into the rolling river.
Dark that hour as Egypt's darkness
Save when lightning pierced the blackness;
Mingled roar of swollen torrent
With the crash of fallen timbers;
Loud the hoarser thunders bellowed;
But above the storm and torrent,
As he hastened up the valley
With the brand of Cain upon him,
Ever in his ear was ringing
That last dying shriek of Laura.
Sank the night behind the mountains
And the sun rolled slowly upward
To a sky by clouds unspotted.
Calmly forward swept the river:
Many a silv'ry laughing cascade
Waved aloft its tiny rainbow;
Through the trees there went a murmur,
Full of peace and full of beauty.
None might think a night so awful
Could precede so fair a dawning.
So the day grew old and older
Till the shadows of the twilight
Gathered round the quiet village,
When a crew of nightly fishers
Found the ghastly form of Laura
Floating in a little eddy
Close beside the village landing.
Many a wild, unfounded rumor,
Many a random, vain conjecture,
Filled the people with excitement;
But at last the fatal whisper
Went abroad, that Norma met her
In the forest by the river.

Some saw Laura leave the village,
Others Norma's late returning;
And the dastard Martin Dumont
Swore he heard their angry talking.
So they forged the chain that bound her,
Link by link they slowly forged it;
Then from home and friends they tore her,
Bore her swiftly to the prison,
To the shadow of the gallows.
Man is even as a vessel
Tossed upon the surging billows
Of a sea of circumstances.
Oft the pirate with his plunder
Finds a cove or sheltered inlet,
While the honest toiling sailor,
Forced to face the raging tempest,
Sinks to rise no more forever.
Came at last the day of judgment.
Many a witness told his story,
As he weeks before had told it.
Last of all the name of Dumont
Sounded through the crowded court-room;
Twice the crier loudly called it,
When from out a shadowed hallway
Slowly stepped a slender maiden,
Stood before the judge and jury,
Pleading to be heard a moment;
So they granted her petition.
Said she, "I am Mabel Dumont,
And the miner was my brother,
But I left him dead this morning.
Yester eve his miner comrades
Bore him bleeding to our cottage,
For a sliding boulder crushed him.

Ere he went he told his story,
Bade me write it as he told it;
When 'twas told, himself he signed it."
Then she handed them the paper,
And they read the miner's story,
All his deathless love for Laura,
All her cruel, idle scorning;
Then he told how he had met her
In the forest by the river,
Told then all the words of Norma
And his vow to hide the murder,
Ending with the declaration,
"By the God of all I swear it,
That 'twas I who murdered Laura,
And no other soul is guilty."
Thus were broken Norma's fetters,
Scattered all the foul suspicion,
And with joy she hastened homeward
Bearing with her fragile Mabel.

As the lily, tempest shattered,
Bends her head in early summer,
Sinking on the sodden bosom
Of the earth she lately gladdened,
So did gentle, patient Mabel,
Crushed beneath the twofold burden
Of her sorrow and dishonor,
Droop while yet her spring was smiling.
All things change, but death may change not
Till the Hand that launched the planets,
And maintains them in their orbits,
Shall stretch forth to stay their motion.
His is one perennial harvest;
Whatsoever Time the sower

Scattereth by the way he treadeth,
Death shall gather soon or later.
All are his—the tender rose-bud
And the hoary giant oak-tree
Both alike await his coming:
From the earth he swiftly bears them
To his distant, silent garner,
And no sound comes o'er the meadows
From the place whence he has borne them.
So he claimed the rancher Gerald,
So he bore him from the bosom
Of the wife he loved so fondly,
And who just as truly loved him.

With her dark-eyed, winsome daughter
Once again she crossed the prairies
To the ivy-mantled cottage
In that far-off eastern valley,
There to wait the Reaper's coming.
Swift her peaceful days flew onward,
Till her threescore years were numbered;
Then as one at even weary
Lays aside her toil for slumber,
Closed her eyes, and widowed Norma
Left the earth she loved forever.
As the fleeting year is changeful
So the life of every man is.
Every season hath its beauties,
Hath its music, lights and shadows;
But the gladdest days that brighten
Are the closing days of Autumn,—
So was closed the life of Norma.

www.ingramcontent.com/pod-product-compliance
Lightning Source LLC
Chambersburg PA
CBHW030345170426
43202CB00010B/1251